CLASSIC COCKTAILS

CLASSIC COCKTAILS

OVER 150 SENSATIONAL DRINK RECIPES SHOWN IN 250 PHOTOGRAPHS

STUART WALTON

southwater

This edition is published by Southwater an imprint of Anness Publishing Ltd Blaby Road, Wigston, Leicestershire LE18 4SE; info@anness.com

www.southwaterbooks.com; www.annesspublishing.com

If you like the images in this book and would liketo investigate using them for publishing, promotionsor advertising, please visit our website www.practicalpictures.com for more information.

A CIP catalogue record for this book is available from the British Library.

Publisher: Joanna Lorenz
Editors: Brian Burns and Kate Eddison
Designer: Nigel Partridge
Photographers: Nicki Dowey, Gus Filgate and Craig Robertson
Additional recipes: Yasuko Fukuoka and Deh-Ta Hsiung
Production Controller: Wendy Lawson

Main image on front cover shows Artists' Special, for recipe see page 76.

PUBLISHER'S NOTE
Although the advice and information in this book are believed to be accurate and true at the time of going to press, neither the authors nor the publisher can accept any legal responsibility or liability for any errors or omissions that may have been made nor for any inaccuracies nor for any loss, harm or injury that comes about from following instructions or advice in this book.

The very young, elderly, pregnant women and those in ill-health or with a compromised immune system are advised against consuming drinks containing raw eggs.

NOTES
Bracketed terms are intended for American readers.
For all recipes, quantities are given in both metric and imperial measures and, where appropriate, in standard cups and spoons. Follow one set of measures, but not a mixture, because they are not interchangeable.
Standard spoon and cup measures are level. 1 tsp = 5ml, 1 tbsp = 15ml, 1 cup = 250ml/8fl oz.
Australian standard tablespoons are 20ml. Australian readers should use 3 tsp in place of 1 tbsp for measuring small quantities.
American pints are 16fl oz/2 cups. American readers should use 20fl oz/ 2.5 cups in place of 1 pint when measuring liquids.
The nutritional analysis given for each recipe is calculated per portion (i.e. serving or item), unless otherwise stated. If the recipe gives a range, such as Serves 4–6, then the nutritional analysis will be for the smaller portion size, i.e. 6 servings. The analysis does not include optional ingredients, such as salt added to taste.
Medium (US large) eggs are used unless otherwise stated.

Contents

Introduction

We may never know at what point in history alcohol was first used to fulfil what would become its time-honoured role as intoxicant. What is certain, however, is that the first such use arose from the discovery of the effects of fermentation on fruit, honey or sticky-sweet palm sap.

First alcohol

The ancient Egyptians used fermented grains for making prototype forms of beer. Wine came after beer, but was to become of crucial cultural and religious importance to the civilizations of Egypt, and classical Greece and Rome. It was used as a sacrament in orgiastic celebrations of the festivals of Dionysos, the Greek god of nature (Bacchus to the Romans).

In addition to its ceremonial and cultural role, wine was also used for culinary purposes. It was capable of making tough meat more supple and removed excess salt from meats that had been preserved. Wine vinegar, its alcohol lost to acetic acid, may have been the first recourse, but wine itself appears in sauce recipes in the historically important late Roman cookbook of Apicius (3rd century AD).

Distillation

The next important step was the discovery of distillation – the extraction of higher alcohols from fermented drinks, using the action of heat to vaporize them. Unlike fermentation, it is a simple process, largely because it is much easier to control.

Alcohol has a lower boiling point than water, so it vaporizes into steam before the water content in the wine starts to boil. When the steam hits a cool surface, it forms a condensation of liquid with a much higher proportion of alcohol than the wine.

Wine was held to have a range of medicinal properties, and the extraction of what was held to be the wine's soul or spirit, through distillation, led to the naming of distillates as 'spirits'.

First distillates

The earliest distillates were of wine, since it had a more salubrious image than beer; grain distillation to produce whiskies and neutral spirits followed in the Middle Ages. Many of these prototypes were flavoured with fruits, herbs or spices, in order to enhance the medicinal properties. The additives also masked the raw taste and off-putting aroma of the unadulterated liquor.

LEFT: *Some cocktails, such as Rocky Mountain, call for specific brands to achieve their unique taste.*

ABOVE: *Enhance the anise flavour in a cocktail by dropping in a whole star anise.*

ABOVE: *Cocktails that do not contain alcohol include this Lemonade on Ice.*

ABOVE: *Cocktails in wonderful colours, such as Rite of Spring, will never fail to impress.*

Spirits

The first spirit to be taken seriously as an object of connoisseurship was probably the brandy of the Cognac region of France. People noticed that the superior, mellower spirit produced by the light wines of Cognac responded particularly well to ageing in oak casks.

Cask-aged spirits derive every aspect of their character from the maturation period they undergo in wood. They do not continue to develop in the bottle.

Scottish and Irish whiskies soon rose to similar prominence. Their differing production processes resulted in distinct regional styles. Many varieties of whisky are made across the world these days.

Liqueurs

Where a distilled drink stops being a spirit and turns into a liqueur is an elusive question. The one constant is that liqueurs have some aromatizing element. Some have histories at least as venerable as cognac and Scotch, such as those produced by the old French monastic orders, such as Bénédictine.

The first and greatest cocktail era, which arrived with the advent of the Jazz Age in the 1920s, rescued many traditional liqueurs from obscurity. The Benedictine monks may be a little shocked to hear of their revered creation being mixed with applejack, gin, apricot brandy and maple syrup, and renamed the Mule's Hind Leg.

How to use this book

The main section of the book consists of over 150 cocktail recipes, arranged by type, so that you can learn how to make a wonderful variety of drinks and happily expand your repertoire. It also includes a fabulous selection of non-alcoholic cocktail recipes.

We will then take a look at what equipment and glasses are needed to make the cocktails and what techniques should be learned, including a detailed guide to making attractive garnishes.

Whether you're throwing a cocktail party or having a quiet drink after work, the drinking world is your oyster. Do it wisely, and have fun.

Gin and Vodka

Of the six basic spirits, gin is the most versatile. It has an assertively perfumed character that enables it to blend well with a range of liqueurs and fruit juices, and even other spirits. Vodka, on the other hand, is a neutral spirit that doesn't interfere with the taste when mixing a range of different flavours. Both colourless, vodka and gin make ideal backgrounds for some flamboyant-looking creations.

Luigi

A 1920s classic, Luigi was created at the Criterion restaurant on London's Piccadilly Circus by one Luigi Naintré. This gin-based cocktail is served in a martini glass, and the addition of a tangerine segment not only makes it look attractive, but enhances the sweet citrus flavour.

MAKES 1 GLASS

1¹/₂ **measures/6 tsp gin**
1¹/₂ **measures/6 tsp dry vermouth**
¹/₄ **measure/1 tsp grenadine**
dash of Cointreau
juice of half a tangerine or
**   mandarin orange**
segment of tangerine, to garnish

1 Shake the liquid ingredients well in a cocktail shaker with ice. Strain into a glass.

2 Add a segment of tangerine to the edge of the glass and serve.

BARTENDING KNOW-HOW
Mandarins and tangerines taste much the same, but the latter are full of pips.

Nutritional information per portion: Energy 125kcal/522kJ; Protein 0.1g; Carbohydrate 7.1g, of which sugars 7.1g; Fat 0g, of which saturates 0g; Cholesterol 0mg; Calcium 3mg; Fibre 0g; Sodium 5mg; Alcohol 14g.

Bennett

Dating from the 1920s, this short drink is sometimes seen spelt with only one 't', and with a small quantity of sugar syrup added to the recipe. This, however, is the original formula, which on the whole I prefer for its sharper, more sophisticated edge.

MAKES 1 GLASS

1¹/₂ measures/6 tsp gin
¹/₂ measure/2 tsp lime juice
2 dashes of Angostura bitters

1 Shake the ingredients well with ice in a cocktail shaker.

2 Strain into a cocktail glass and serve.

Nutritional information per portion: Energy 51kcal/211kJ; Protein 0g; Carbohydrate 0.2g, of which sugars 0.2g; Fat 0g, of which saturates 0g; Cholesterol 0mg; Calcium 1mg; Fibre 0g; Sodium 0mg; Alcohol 7.3g.

Gin Fizz

The combination of sourness and fizziness in this 19th-century recipe makes this cocktail really refreshing. Perfect for a summer's day, serve this long drink in a frosted, tall glass with plenty of ice and add as much soda water as you like.

MAKES 1 GLASS

2 measures/3 tbsp gin
juice of half a large lemon
5ml/1 tsp caster (superfine) sugar
soda water

1 Shake the gin, lemon juice and sugar with ice until the sugar is properly dissolved.

2 Pour out into a frosted, tall, narrow glass half-filled with ice.

3 Top up the glass with soda water.

BARTENDING KNOW-HOW
There should ideally be a little less soda water than the other combined ingredients, but it is very much a matter of personal taste.

Nutritional information per portion: Energy 117kcal/485kJ; Protein 0.1g; Carbohydrate 4.4g, of which sugars 4.4g; Fat 0g, of which saturates 0g; Cholesterol 0mg; Calcium 3mg; Fibre 0g; Sodium 0mg; Alcohol 14.3g.

Tom Collins

This is similar to a Gin Fizz, except that it isn't shaken and tends to be made with a little less soda. Originally known as John Collins, after the head waiter at a London hotel in the early 19th century, it changed its name when it began to be made with the Old Tom brand of gin.

MAKES 1 GLASS

2 measures / 3 tbsp gin
juice of half a large lemon
5ml / 1 tsp sugar
soda water
slice of lemon, to garnish

1 Half-fill a frosted, tall glass with ice. Pour in the gin and lemon juice.

2 Add the sugar and stir to dissolve.

3 Add roughly a measure and a half of soda, a slice of lemon and a couple of straws, and serve.

BARTENDING KNOW-HOW
The invention of gin is apocryphally credited to one Franciscus de la Boë, a medical professor at the University of Leiden in the Netherlands, sometime in the mid-17th century. Even if he is the true progenitor of gin, however, he was almost certainly not the first to add juniper berries for medicinal reasons to a pure distilled spirit. The 12th-century monastery at Salerno, where European distillation was born, is the most likely origin of the basic recipe.

Nutritional information per portion: Energy 116kcal/483kJ; Protein 0g; Carbohydrate 4.3g, of which sugars 4.3g; Fat 0g, of which saturates 0g; Cholesterol 0mg; Calcium 3mg; Fibre 0g; Sodium 0mg; Alcohol 14.3g.

Gin Swizzle

The Swizzle dates from the early 19th century, and was originally a drink made frothy purely by energetic stirring. The implement used for this, known as the swizzle-stick, took its name from the drink. Serve this zingy cocktail in a tall glass.

MAKES 1 GLASS

2 measures/3 tbsp gin
1/4 measure/1 tsp sugar syrup
juice of a lime
2 dashes of Angostura bitters

1 Beat all the ingredients together (as if you were preparing eggs for an omelette) in a large jug (pitcher), with ice.

2 When the drink is good and foaming, strain it into a tall glass. Alternatively, you can make the drink in the tall glass, but remember to stir it up vigorously with a swizzle-stick.

BARTENDING KNOW-HOW
Some recipes add soda water to achieve the swizzle effect, but originally it was all done by elbow grease. The froth will subside fairly quickly anyway.

Nutritional information per portion: Energy 124kcal/517kJ; Protein 0.1g; Carbohydrate 6.4g, of which sugars 6.4g; Fat 0g, of which saturates 0g; Cholesterol 0mg; Calcium 4mg; Fibre 0g; Sodium 0mg; Alcohol 14.3g.

Gin Sour

The Sour dates from the 1850s, and can be made with any of the basic spirits. Fresh lemon juice is naturally the key to it, with the edge taken off it by means of a pinch of sugar. However, it should never taste at all sweet, otherwise it wouldn't be worthy of its name.

MAKES 1 GLASS

2 measures/3 tbsp gin
juice of half a large lemon
5ml/1 tsp caster (superfine) sugar

1 Shake all the ingredients together with ice in a cocktail shaker.

2 Strain the drink into a rocks glass or small tumbler.

BARTENDING KNOW-HOW
Some bartenders add the briefest squirt of soda just before serving for extra pep, but it is better served wholly still.

Nutritional information per portion: Energy 116kcal/483kJ; Protein 0g; Carbohydrate 4.3g, of which sugars 4.3g; Fat 0g, of which saturates 0g; Cholesterol 0mg; Calcium 3mg; Fibre 0g; Sodium 0mg; Alcohol 14.3g.

Honolulu

This fruity little shooter should be served in a shot glass. The mixture of tropical flavours in the drink is probably what led to the name.

MAKES 1 GLASS

1 measure/1¹/₂ tbsp gin
¹/₄ measure/1 tsp pineapple juice
¹/₄ measure/1 tsp orange juice
¹/₄ measure/1 tsp lemon juice
¹/₄ measure/1 tsp pineapple syrup
   (from a can)
1 drop of Angostura bitters

1 Shake all but the last ingredient with ice in a cocktail shaker.

2 Strain into a shot glass.

3 Add a single drop of Angostura to the drink, and knock back in one.

Nutritional information per portion: Energy 60kcal/248kJ;
Protein 0.1g; Carbohydrate 1g, of which sugars 1g;
Fat 0g, of which saturates 0g; Cholesterol 0mg;
Calcium 1mg; Fibre 0g; Sodium 1mg; Alcohol 7.9g.

Carla

This fruity concoction owes its character to Dutch genever, which should be used in preference to ordinary London gin.

MAKES 1 GLASS

1½ measures/6 tsp jonge genever
2 measures/3 tbsp orange juice
1 measure/1½ tbsp passion fruit juice
2 measures/3 tbsp lemonade
slice of orange, to garnish (optional)

1 Shake the first three ingredients together with a couple of handfuls of crushed ice in a cocktail shaker.

2 Pour the drink, unstrained, into a highball glass.

3 Add the lemonade. Garnish with a slice of orange, if you like.

BARTENDING KNOW-HOW
In the Netherlands, genever is nearly always drunk neat, accompanied by a chaser of the local beer.

Nutritional information per portion: Energy 79kcal/328kJ;
Protein 0.3g; Carbohydrate 7.2g, of which sugars 7.2g;
Fat 0.1g, of which saturates 0g; Cholesterol 0mg;
Calcium 8mg; Fibre 0g; Sodium 8mg; Alcohol 7.2g.

My Fair Lady

This frothy, fruity cocktail (pictured right) was invented at London's Savoy Hotel in the 1950s to coincide with a production of the much-loved Lerner and Loewe musical based on George Bernard Shaw's play Pygmalion.

MAKES 1 GLASS

1 measure/1½ tbsp gin
½ measure/2 tsp orange juice
½ measure/2 tsp lemon juice
¼ measure/1 tsp crème de fraise
1 egg white
slice of orange, to garnish (optional)

1 Shake the gin, orange juice, lemon juice, crème de fraise and egg white thoroughly with ice in a cocktail shaker.

2 Strain into a cocktail glass.

3 Skewer a slice of orange on a cocktail stick (toothpick) and use to garnish the rim of the glass, if you like.

Nutritional information per portion: Energy 76kcal/318kJ; Protein 3g; Carbohydrate 2.4g, of which sugars 2.4g; Fat 0g, of which saturates 0g; Cholesterol 0mg; Calcium 4mg; Fibre 0g; Sodium 62mg; Alcohol 7.9g.

Horse's Neck

The name derives from the shape of the lemon rind that hangs in the glass. There are various versions of this mix, the earliest using bourbon or brandy, but gin eventually became the most popular. Serve in a Collins glass.

MAKES 1 GLASS

1 lemon
2 measures/3 tbsp gin
dry ginger ale

1 Cut the entire rind from a lemon, spiral-fashion. Dangle it from the rim of a tall glass so that it hangs down inside.

2 Add plenty of cracked ice and the gin, and then top up with ginger ale.

BARTENDING KNOW-HOW
You can also add a dash of Angostura bitters to this cocktail, if the mood takes you, but it is by no means essential.

Nutritional information per portion: Energy 115kcal/476kJ; Protein 0g; Carbohydrate 3.9g, of which sugars 3.9g; Fat 0g, of which saturates 0g; Cholesterol 0mg; Calcium 0mg; Fibre 0g; Sodium 0mg; Alcohol 14.3g.

Damn the Weather

This cocktail has been around since the 1920s, and the name presumably commemorates a particularly persistent gloomy spell of weather.

MAKES 1 GLASS

1 measure/1¹/₂ tbsp gin
¹/₂ measure/2 tsp sweet red vermouth
¹/₂ measure/2 tsp orange juice
¹/₄ measure/1 tsp orange curaçao
orange rind, to garnish

1 Shake the liquid ingredients well with ice in a cocktail shaker.

2 Strain the drink into a chilled whisky tumbler.

3 Add a twist of orange rind, wrapped around a cocktail stick (toothpick), to garnish.

Nutritional information per portion: Energy 78kcal/322kJ;
Protein 0.1g; Carbohydrate 2.8g, of which sugars 2.8g;
Fat 0g, of which saturates 0g; Cholesterol 0mg;
Calcium 2mg; Fibre 0g; Sodium 3mg; Alcohol 9.6g.

Cloister

A strong lemony/herbal flavour pervades the Cloister. It is a short drink that delivers a strong kick-start to the tastebuds with the zing of lemon and grapefruit.

MAKES 1 GLASS

1¹/₂ measures/6 tsp gin
¹/₂ measure/2 tsp yellow Chartreuse
¹/₂ measure/2 tsp grapefruit juice
¹/₄ measure/1 tsp lemon juice
¹/₄ measure/1 tsp sugar syrup
grapefruit rind, to garnish

1 Shake all the liquid ingredients well with ice in a cocktail shaker.

2 Strain into a cocktail glass.

3 Garnish with a twist of grapefruit rind and serve.

Nutritional information per portion: Energy 127kcal/531kJ; Protein 0.1g; Carbohydrate 9.4g, of which sugars 9.4g; Fat 0g, of which saturates 0g; Cholesterol 0mg; Calcium 5mg; Fibre 0g; Sodium 2mg; Alcohol 13.1g.

Gin Smash

Try this cocktail with any fresh mint you can find: peppermint and spearmint would each contribute their own flavour to this simple and very refreshing summery drink.

MAKES 1 GLASS

15ml/1 tbsp sugar
4 sprigs fresh mint
2 measures/3 tbsp gin

1 Dissolve the sugar in a little water in the cocktail shaker.

2 Add the mint and, using a muddler, bruise and press the juices out of the leaves.

3 Add plenty of crushed ice and finally the gin. Shake for about 20 seconds.

4 Strain into a small wine glass filled with crushed ice.

Nutritional information per portion: Energy 158kcal/663kJ; Protein 0.5g; Carbohydrate 16.2g, of which sugars 15.7g; Fat 0.1g, of which saturates 0g; Cholesterol 0mg; Calcium 29mg; Fibre 0g; Sodium 2mg; Alcohol 16g.

Dundee

What else but Scottish ingredients (two of them, in fact) could give a drink a name like this? This is a dry, sour cocktail, which gives quite a kick.

MAKES 1 GLASS

1 measure/1¹/₂ tbsp gin
³/₄ measure/3 tsp Scotch
¹/₂ measure/2 tsp Drambuie
¹/₂ measure/2 tsp lemon juice
lemon rind, to garnish

1 Shake all the liquid ingredients well with ice in a cocktail shaker.

2 Strain into a whisky tumbler.

3 Squeeze a twist of lemon rind over the drink and then drop it into the glass.

Nutritional information per portion: Energy 116kcal/484kJ; Protein 0g; Carbohydrate 2.6g, of which sugars 2.6g; Fat 0g, of which saturates 0g; Cholesterol 0mg; Calcium 1mg; Fibre 0g; Sodium 1mg; Alcohol 15.3g.

Gin and Lemon Fizz

If gin and tonic is your tipple, try this chilled alternative. The fruit and flower ice cubes make a lively decoration for any iced drink. This recipe serves two.

MAKES 2 GLASSES

mixture of small edible berries or currants
pieces of thinly pared lemon or orange rind
tiny edible flowers
4 scoops of lemon sorbet
30ml/2 tbsp gin
120ml/4fl oz chilled tonic water

1 To make the decorated ice cubes, place each fruit, piece of rind or flower in a section of an ice-cube tray. Fill with water and freeze for several hours until the cubes are solid.

2 Divide the sorbet into two cocktail glasses or use small tumblers, with a capacity of about 150ml/¼ pint.

3 Spoon over the gin and add a couple of the ornamental ice cubes to each glass. Top up with tonic water and serve immediately.

BARTENDING KNOW-HOW
When making the ice cubes, choose small herb flowers such as borage or mint, or edible flowers such as rose geraniums, primulas or rose buds.

Nutritional information per portion: Energy 368kcal/ 1569kJ; Protein 1.8g; Carbohydrate 79g, of which sugars 68.4g; Fat 0g, of which saturates 0g; Cholesterol 0mg; Calcium 5mg; Fibre 0g; Sodium 41mg; Alcohol 9.6g.

Whiteout

A highly indulgent preparation with which to conclude the gin collection, this is a sweet, chocolate cream cocktail that tastes far more innocuous than it actually is.

MAKES 1 GLASS

1½ measures/6 tsp gin
1 measure/1½ tbsp white crème
  de cacao
1 measure/1½ tbsp double
  (heavy) cream
white chocolate, to garnish

1 Shake all the liquid ingredients very well with ice in a cocktail shaker to amalgamate the cream fully.

2 Strain into a chilled cocktail glass.

3 Grate a small piece of white chocolate over the surface.

BARTENDING KNOW-HOW
It is estimated that, at the time the Gin Act was introduced in 1736, average consumption in London had hit something like two-thirds of a bottle per head per day.

Nutritional information per portion: Energy 258kcal/ 1067kJ; Protein 0.4g; Carbohydrate 5.5g, of which sugars 5.5g; Fat 15.6g, of which saturates 7.5g; Cholesterol 31mg; Calcium 15mg; Fibre 0g; Sodium 25mg; Alcohol 13.4g.

Monkey Gland

From the classic cocktail era of the early 1920s, this drink (pictured right) was created at Ciro's Club in London, a legendary jazz nightspot just off the Charing Cross Road. The head bartender, Harry McElhone, later moved to Paris and ran Harry's New York Bar, where he ascended to true international renown.

MAKES 1 GLASS

2 measures/3 tbsp gin
1 measure/1¹/₂ tbsp orange juice
¹/₂ measure/2 tsp grenadine
¹/₂ measure/2 tsp absinthe
slice of orange, to garnish

1 Shake all the liquid ingredients with plenty of ice in a cocktail shaker.

2 Strain into a large wine glass.

3 Garnish with a slice of orange.

Nutritional information per portion: Energy 178kcal/737kJ; Protein 0.1g; Carbohydrate 4.4g, of which sugars 4.4g; Fat 0g, of which saturates 0g; Cholesterol 0mg; Calcium 3mg; Fibre 0g; Sodium 3mg; Alcohol 22.9g.

Amsterdam

This deliciously orangey cocktail is unusual in having the ice left in it. It was invented in the city whose name it bears. Squeeze a fresh mandarin and use fresh segments if you have one, but you could also use canned mandarin segments and the unsweetened juice from the can, if you prefer.

MAKES 1 GLASS

1¹/₂ measures/6 tsp gin
¹/₂ measure/2 tsp Cointreau
³/₄ measure/3 tsp mandarin juice
mandarin segments, to garnish

1 Shake the gin, Cointreau and mandarin juice with cracked ice in a cocktail shaker.

2 Pour, without straining, into a rocks glass.

3 Add one or two mandarin segments to the glass and serve.

Nutritional information per portion: Energy 109kcal/455kJ; Protein 0.1g; Carbohydrate 5.4g, of which sugars 5.4g; Fat 0g, of which saturates 0g; Cholesterol 0mg; Calcium 4mg; Fibre 0.1g; Sodium 3mg; Alcohol 12.6g.

Red Cloud

Although red clouds at night were once said to be a sailor's delight, you don't have to be ocean-bound to enjoy one of these. This classic 1920s cocktail is a refreshing drink with a sharp kick provided by the lemon juice. Serve in a cocktail glass or champagne saucer.

MAKES 1 GLASS

1^1/$_2$ measures/6 tsp gin
^{3}/$_4$ measure/3 tsp apricot brandy
^{1}/$_2$ measure/2 tsp lemon juice
^{1}/$_4$ measure/1 tsp grenadine
dash of Angostura bitters
half slice of lemon and a cherry,
      to garnish

1 Shake all the liquid ingredients well with ice in a cocktail shaker.

2 Strain into a champagne saucer or cocktail glass.

3 Garnish with a half-slice of lemon and a cherry.

BARTENDING KNOW-HOW
The oversized label around each Angostura bitters bottle was an administrative error that just stuck!

Nutritional information per portion: Energy 118kcal/ 492kJ; Protein 0g; Carbohydrate 6.5g, of which sugars 6.5g; Fat 0g, of which saturates 0g; Cholesterol 0mg; Calcium 0mg; Fibre 0g; Sodium 1mg; Alcohol 13.3g.

Maiden's Blush

There were two quite distinct recipes for Maiden's Blush, even in the 1920s. The first mixed gin with orange curaçao, lemon juice and grenadine. This one was a slightly more lethal proposition, and the blush effect in the colour is more apparent, if you need any excuse to up the ante.

MAKES 1 GLASS

2 measures/3 tbsp gin
1 measure/1¹/₂ tbsp absinthe
¹/₄ measure/1 tsp grenadine

1 Shake all the ingredients well with ice in a cocktail shaker.

2 Strain the drink into an ice-cold cocktail glass.

BARTENDING KNOW-HOW
Cocktails containing absinthe should be served sparingly. Too many aren't necessarily very nice.

Nutritional information per portion: Energy 213kcal/882kJ; Protein 0g; Carbohydrate 1.6g, of which sugars 1.6g; Fat 0g, of which saturates 0g; Cholesterol 0mg; Calcium 0mg; Fibre 0g; Sodium 1mg; Alcohol 29.6g.

Vunderful

A long, lazy Sunday afternoon tipple, conjured up in the heat of southern Africa. Leave the fruits in the gin for as long as possible. This recipe contains 20 servings.

MAKES 20 GLASSES

400g/14oz can lychees
2 peaches, sliced
3/4 bottle gin

FOR EACH SERVING YOU WILL NEED:
1 measure/1 1/2 tbsp Pimm's
2–3 dashes Angostura bitters
5 measures/120ml/4fl oz chilled tonic water or lemonade
half-slice of lime, to garnish

1 Strain the lychees from the syrup and place them in a wide-necked jar with the peach slices and the gin. Leave overnight or for anything up to a month.

2 For each serving, mix in a large jug (pitcher) a measure of the lychee gin with the Pimm's and the bitters to taste. Strain into tall tumblers filled with ice cubes.

3 Add chilled tonic water or lemonade to top up. Put a couple of the drained gin-soaked lychees and peach slices into each glass, stirring and crushing the fruit with a muddler. Add a half-slice of lime to the rim of each glass.

Nutritional information per portion: Energy 115kcal/489kJ; Protein 0.2g; Carbohydrate 22.2g, of which sugars 11.7g; Fat 0g, of which saturates 0g; Cholesterol 0mg; Calcium 4mg; Fibre 0.3g; Sodium 8mg; Alcohol 4.4g.

Juan-les-Pins

Once the preferred destination of the Mediterranean jet-set, the Riviera resort is fittingly honoured by this appetizing mixture of gin, an aperitif and a liqueur.

MAKES 1 GLASS

1 measure/1½ tbsp gin
¾ measure/3 tsp white Dubonnet
½ measure/2 tsp apricot brandy
dash of lemon juice
slice of apricot and a cherry, to garnish

1 Shake all the liquid ingredients well with ice in a cocktail shaker.

2 Strain into a cocktail glass.

3 Garnish the drink with a slice of apricot and a cherry speared by a cocktail stick (toothpick).

Nutritional information per portion: Energy 153kcal/640kJ; Protein 0g; Carbohydrate 13.1g, of which sugars 13.1g; Fat 0g, of which saturates 0g; Cholesterol 0mg; Calcium 1mg; Fibre 0g; Sodium 2mg; Alcohol 14.9g.

RAC

This cocktail (pictured right) was created on the eve of the First World War by the barman of the Royal Automobile Club in London's Pall Mall.

MAKES 1 GLASS

1¹/₂ measures/6 tsp gin
³/₄ measure/3 tsp dry vermouth
³/₄ measure/3 tsp sweet red vermouth
¹/₄ measure/1 tsp orange bitters
orange rind

1 Shake the liquid ingredients with ice in a cocktail shaker.

2 Strain into a glass.

3 Squeeze a twist of orange rind over the top of the drink to release its oil.

Nutritional information per portion: Energy 99kcal/412kJ; Protein 0g; Carbohydrate 0.9g, of which sugars 0.9g; Fat 0g, of which saturates 0g; Cholesterol 0mg; Calcium 2mg; Fibre 0g; Sodium 3mg; Alcohol 13.7g.

Little Red Riding Hood

Vivid summery fruit flavours make a cocktail that tastes as innocent as Grandma, but has a bite more reminiscent of the Wolf!

MAKES 1 GLASS

1 measure/1¹/₂ tbsp gin
³/₄ measure/3 tsp crème de mûre
³/₄ measure/3 tsp crème de fraise
1¹/₂ measures/6 tsp orange juice
strawberry, blackberry and cherry, to garnish

1 Shake the liquid ingredients with ice in a cocktail shaker.

2 Strain into a large cocktail glass filled with crushed ice.

3 Garnish the drink with a strawberry, a blackberry and a cherry.

Nutritional information per portion: Energy 139kcal/582kJ; Protein 0.1g; Carbohydrate 12.5g, of which sugars 12.5g; Fat 0g, of which saturates 0g; Cholesterol 0mg; Calcium 5mg; Fibre 0g; Sodium 7mg; Alcohol 13.1g.

Boyar

This very dry and herb-tinged mixture would make a good appetite-whetter at a party where nibbles are going to be served. The tiny quantity of kümmel shines through, and leaves a very appetizing aftertaste in its wake.

MAKES 1 GLASS

2 measures/3 tbsp vodka
¹/₂ measure/2 tsp dry vermouth
¹/₄ measure/1 tsp kümmel

1 Shake the ingredients with ice in a cocktail shaker.

2 Strain into a cocktail glass. This drink doesn't need a garnish.

BARTENDING KNOW-HOW

The kümmel you will buy for making a Boyar will most probably be the pre-eminent Wolfschmidt brand. It has been sold in the UK since the late Victorian era, having originally made its name in the Baltic state of Latvia.

Nutritional information per portion: Energy 124kcal/514kJ; Protein 0g; Carbohydrate 1.9g, of which sugars 1.9g; Fat 0g, of which saturates 0g; Cholesterol 0mg; Calcium 1mg; Fibre 0g; Sodium 2mg; Alcohol 16.7g.

Blue Shark

Blue curaçao mixes so well with clear spirits that it would seem a shame not to include a vodka-based recipe, and here is a popular American one. Serve this cocktail simply in an old-fashioned rocks glass – no garnish is needed for this stunningly coloured drink.

MAKES 1 GLASS

1 measure/1¹/₂ tbsp vodka
1 measure/1¹/₂ tbsp tequila
¹/₂ measure/2 tsp blue curaçao
orange rind

1 Shake all the liquid ingredients well with ice in a cocktail shaker.

2 Strain into a small rocks glass.

3 Squeeze a little orange rind over the drink to release the oil, but don't add the rind itself.

Nutritional information per portion: Energy 118kcal/491kJ; Protein 0g; Carbohydrate 1.8g, of which sugars 1.8g; Fat 0g, of which saturates 0g; Cholesterol 0mg; Calcium 0mg; Fibre 0g; Sodium 0mg; Alcohol 4.4g.

Green Dragon

You will find one glass of this dry, savoury and extremely strong cocktail is more than enough. Sip it slowly, or be brave and take it at a couple of gulps. Then lie down.

MAKES 1 GLASS

2 measures/3 tbsp Stolichnaya vodka
1 measure/1½ tbsp green Chartreuse
cocktail onion, to garnish

1 Shake the liquid ingredients well with ice in a cocktail shaker.

2 Strain into a cocktail glass and garnish with the cocktail onion.

Nutritional information per portion: Energy 171kcal/709kJ; Protein 0g; Carbohydrate 5.5g, of which sugars 5.5g; Fat 0g, of which saturates 0g; Cholesterol 0mg; Calcium 0mg; Fibre 0g; Sodium 1mg; Alcohol 21.4g.

French Horn

The drink is so called because it calls for a particular variety of French liqueur called Chambord, made from black raspberries. If you can't find it, substitute ordinary crème de framboise.

MAKES 1 GLASS

1 measure/1¹/₂ tbsp vodka
³/₄ measure/3 tsp Chambord
   (or crème de framboise)
¹/₂ measure/2 tsp lemon juice
raspberry, to garnish

1 Stir the liquid ingredients in a jug (pitcher) with plenty of ice.

2 Strain into a cocktail glass and garnish with a whole raspberry.

Nutritional information per portion: Energy 90kcal/375kJ; Protein 0g; Carbohydrate 5.1g, of which sugars 5.1g; Fat 0g, of which saturates 0g; Cholesterol 0mg; Calcium 1mg; Fibre 0g; Sodium 2mg; Alcohol 10.1g.

Screwdriver

The Screwdriver is the original vodka and orange, so named – as the story has it – after an American oil-rig worker developed the habit of stirring his drink with a screwdriver. As a member of the classic cocktail repertoire, it probably only dates from the 1950s, which is when vodka made its first, tentative appearance on Western markets. The rest is history.

MAKES 1 GLASS

2 measures/3 tbsp vodka
4 measures/6 tbsp orange juice
slice of orange, to garnish

1 Add the ingredients, spirit first, to a rocks glass or whisky tumbler loaded with ice cubes, and throw in a slice of orange.

BARTENDING KNOW-HOW
Freshly squeezed juice gives a grown-up taste and appears to pack more of a punch, as the juice is naturally thinner than concentrated orange juice from a carton.

Nutritional information per portion: Energy 132kcal/551kJ; Protein 0.5g; Carbohydrate 7.9g, of which sugars 7.9g; Fat 0.1g, of which saturates 0g; Cholesterol 0mg; Calcium 9mg; Fibre 0.1g; Sodium 9mg; Alcohol 14.3g.

Harvey Wallbanger

This is the next step up from a Screwdriver, with a dash of Galliano added. It is a 1970s recipe that supposedly derives its name from having left a gentleman called Harvey, who had downed several of them, in the walking-into-walls state. There is no need to go quite that far, but it's easy to see why the formula became such a popular one in nightclubs.

MAKES 1 GLASS

2 measures/3 tbsp vodka
³/₄ measure/3 tsp Galliano
5 measures/120ml/4fl oz orange juice
half-slice of orange, to garnish

1 Add the vodka and orange juice to a highball glass half-filled with cracked ice.

2 Pour the Galliano carefully over so that it floats on top.

3 Garnish with a half-slice of orange, decorated with a canelle knife.

Nutritional information per portion: Energy 182kcal/762kJ; Protein 0.6g; Carbohydrate 15.5g, of which sugars 15.5g; Fat 0.1g, of which saturates 0g; Cholesterol 0mg; Calcium 13mg; Fibre 0.1g; Sodium 14mg; Alcohol 17.3g.

Balalaika

A recipe from the age when vodka was still enough of a commercial novelty for a drink containing it to be given a name with glamorous connotations. It has a mild spirit flavour due to the vodka, and sharp citrus flavours from the lemon juice.

MAKES 1 GLASS

1¹/₂ **measures/6 tsp vodka**
³/₄ **measure/3 tsp Cointreau**
³/₄ **measure/3 tsp lemon juice**
slice of orange and a cherry, to garnish

1 Shake the liquid ingredients well with plenty of ice in a cocktail shaker.

2 Strain into a cocktail glass.

3 Add an orange-and-cherry garnish.

Nutritional information per portion: Energy 115kcal/477kJ; Protein 0g; Carbohydrate 3.9g, of which sugars 3.9g; Fat 0g, of which saturates 0g; Cholesterol 0mg; Calcium 1mg; Fibre 0g; Sodium 1mg; Alcohol 14.3g.

Blenheim

A twist on the basic Black Russian idea, Blenheim uses orange juice instead of cola, if you want a non-alcoholic mixer in there. The resulting colour is not particularly attractive, but don't be put off – the flavour is better than it looks.

MAKES 1 GLASS

1¹/₂ measures/6 tsp vodka
³/₄ measure/3 tsp Tia Maria
³/₄ measure/3 tsp orange juice
physalis, to garnish

1 Shake all the ingredients well with ice in a cocktail shaker.

2 Strain into a cocktail glass and garnish with a physalis.

Nutritional information per portion: Energy 119kcal/496kJ; Protein 0.1g; Carbohydrate 5g, of which sugars 5g; Fat 0g, of which saturates 0g; Cholesterol 0mg; Calcium 2mg; Fibre 0g; Sodium 2mg; Alcohol 14.3g.

Dickson's Bloody Mary

This recipe has plenty of spicy character, with horseradish, sherry and Tabasco. Made with chilli or pepper vodka, this hot and piquant drink has a real kick to it.

MAKES 1 GLASS

2 measures/3 tbsp chilli-flavoured vodka
1 measure/1¹/₂ tbsp fino sherry
7 measures/150ml/¹/₄ pint tomato juice
1 measure/1¹/₂ tbsp lemon juice
2–3 dashes Tabasco
10–15ml/2–3 tsp Worcestershire sauce
2.5ml/¹/₂ tsp creamed horseradish
5ml/1 tsp celery salt
salt and ground black pepper
celery stalk, pitted green olives and a
     cherry tomato, to garnish

1 Fill a pitcher with cracked ice and add the vodka, sherry and tomato juice. Stir well.

2 Add the lemon juice, Tabasco, Worcestershire sauce and horseradish. Stir again.

3 Add the celery salt, salt and pepper, and stir until the pitcher has frosted and the contents are chilled.

4 Strain into a tall tumbler, half-filled with ice cubes. Add a stick of celery, and the olives and tomato skewered on to a cocktail stick (toothpick).

Nutritional information per portion: Energy 150kcal/628kJ;
Protein 1.1g; Carbohydrate 4.8g, of which sugars 4.7g;
Fat 0.4g, of which saturates 0.1g; Cholesterol 1mg;
Calcium 16mg; Fibre 0.8g; Sodium 324mg; Alcohol 17.9g.

Black Cossack

You may think its presence will hardly be noticed, but the extra kick given to the beer by the slug of vodka in a Black Cossack is an appreciable one.

MAKES 1 GLASS

1 measure/1¹/₂ tbsp vodka
300ml/¹/₂ pint Guinness

1 Pour a measure of ice-cold vodka into a highball or half-pint glass.

2 Add the well-chilled Guinness.

3 Wait for the head on the beer to settle before drinking.

Nutritional information per portion: Energy 140kcal/
585kJ; Protein 1.2g; Carbohydrate 4.5g, of which
sugars 4.5g; Fat 0g, of which saturates 0g;
Cholesterol 0mg; Calcium 12mg; Fibre 0g; Sodium 18mg;
Alcohol 17g.

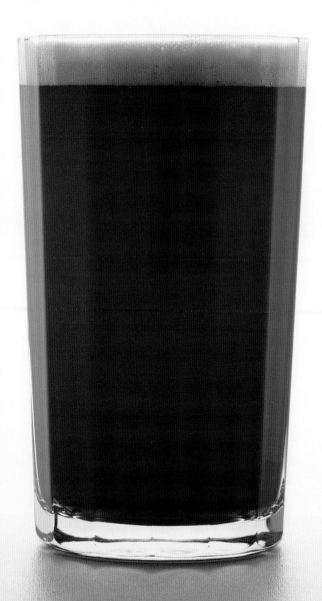

Slow Comfortable Screw

The 1970s idea of a joke in the drink's name may be a touch embarrassing now, but the mixture is a good one, and the drink was something of a modern classic a generation ago.

MAKES 1 GLASS

1 measure/1¹/₂ tbsp vodka
³/₄ measure/3 tsp Southern Comfort
³/₄ measure/3 tsp sloe gin
5 measures/120ml/4fl oz orange juice
cocktail cherry, to garnish

1 Add the vodka, Southern Comfort and sloe gin to a highball glass half-packed with ice.

2 Stir to combine, and then top up with the orange juice.

3 Garnish with a cherry on a cocktail stick (toothpick) and a plastic novelty.

Nutritional information per portion: Energy 180kcal/752kJ; Protein 0.6g; Carbohydrate 19.1g, of which sugars 19.1g; Fat 0.1g, of which saturates 0g; Cholesterol 0mg; Calcium 13mg; Fibre 0.1g; Sodium 15mg; Alcohol 14.8g.

Black Russian

The true Black Russian is simply equal measures of vodka and Tia Maria, or Kahlúa, mixed with ice cubes in a tumbler. However, the fashion in recent years has been to serve it as a long drink in a big glass, topped up with cola.

MAKES 1 GLASS

1 measure/1¹/₂ tbsp vodka
1 measure/1¹/₂ tbsp Tia Maria

1 Add the spirits to a tumbler with ice and stir well.

Nutritional information per portion: Energy 158kcal/663kJ; Protein 0g; Carbohydrate 20.5g, of which sugars 20.5g; Fat 0g, of which saturates 0g; Cholesterol 0mg; Calcium 8mg; Fibre 0g; Sodium 9mg; Alcohol 11.6g.

BARTENDING KNOW-HOW
Proportions vary according to taste. Two parts vodka to one part Tia Maria on ice, with no mixer, makes a very adult drink. Some people insist on Kahlúa rather than Tia Maria with the vodka. Either way, it is best not to adulterate the drink with cola.

Rum and Tequila

Before the advent of vodka cocktails, rum

was the spirit with which all the exotic

flavours were mixed. There are three grades

in the cocktail repertoire: white, light (or

golden) and dark. A more recent commercial

phenomenon than vodka, tequila has acquired

comparatively few cocktail recipes. It mixes

well with fruit juices, but combinations with

liqueurs are still developing, giving an

experimental quality to some of the recipes.

Tom and Jerry

A cold weather drink invented in the 1850s by the legendary Jerry Thomas of St Louis, Missouri, Tom and Jerry is one of the oldest cocktails in this book. It is said that Mr Thomas would serve these at the first snows of winter. This recipe serves four to six people.

MAKES 4–6 GLASSES

FOR THE BATTER

3 eggs
45ml/3 tbsp caster (superfine) sugar
pinch bicarbonate of soda (baking soda)
1 measure/1¹/₂ tbsp dark rum
1.5ml/¹/₄ tsp ground cinnamon
pinch ground cloves
pinch allspice
nutmeg, to garnish

FOR EACH DRINK

1 measure/1¹/₂ tbsp dark rum
1 measure/1¹/₂ tbsp brandy
4 measures/6 tbsp boiling milk

1 Separate the eggs and beat the whites into stiff peaks, adding 15ml/1 tbsp of the sugar with the bicarbonate.

2 Mix the yolks separately with the rum, the rest of the sugar and the spices. Then fold in the whites with a metal spoon.

3 Using heatproof glasses, put in 15ml/1 tbsp of the batter and 1 measure/1¹/₂ tbsp each of rum and brandy, then top up with boiled milk.

4 Dust with nutmeg and serve.

Nutritional information per portion: Energy 216kcal/903kJ; Protein 6.2g; Carbohydrate 12.1g, of which sugars 12.1g; Fat 4.3g, of which saturates 1.7g; Cholesterol 100mg; Calcium 126mg; Fibre 0g; Sodium 74mg; Alcohol 15.4g.

Daiquiri

The Daiquiri is one of the most adapted and abused cocktails in the repertoire. Created in the 1890s, it is named after a town in Cuba and was originally nothing more than a white rum sour. Despite its extreme simplicity, this really is one of the all-time perfect cocktail recipes.

MAKES 1 GLASS

2 measures/3 tbsp white rum
juice of half a lime or a quarter of a lemon
5ml/1 tsp caster (superfine) sugar

1 Shake all the ingredients well with ice in a cocktail shaker to dissolve the caster sugar.

2 Strain into a well-chilled cocktail glass. Serve ungarnished.

Nutritional information per portion: Energy 120kcal/498kJ; Protein 0g; Carbohydrate 5.2g, of which sugars 5.2g; Fat 0g, of which saturates 0g; Cholesterol 0mg; Calcium 3mg; Fibre 0g; Sodium 0mg; Alcohol 14.3g.

Ti Punch

This is a great favourite in the originally French Caribbean islands. The 'ti' is short for the French word 'petit' meaning this cocktail is affectionately titled 'little punch'. Don't let the name fool you, though – this cocktail can pack quite a punch.

MAKES 1 GLASS

1 lime
2 measures/3 tbsp French Caribbean
    white rum
¼ measure/1 tsp sugar syrup

1 Reserve one slice of lime, then cut the rest of the lime into wedges and put them in a wide-based rocks glass.

2 Pound and crush them with a blunt instrument to release the juices, but leave all the residue in the glass.

3 Add the syrup and the rum, and plenty of cracked ice. Garnish with the reserved lime slice.

Nutritional information per portion: Energy 124kcal/514kJ; Protein 0g; Carbohydrate 6.3g, of which sugars 6.3g; Fat 0g, of which saturates 0g; Cholesterol 0mg; Calcium 3mg; Fibre 0g; Sodium 0mg; Alcohol 14.3g.

Cuba Libre

This is a brand-specific cocktail if ever there was one. Created in Cuba – where Bacardi was then produced – in the late 19th century, the novelty value of Cuba Libre lay in its use of Coca-cola, a newfangled tonic beverage, then less than ten years on the market.

MAKES 1 GLASS

juice and rind of half a lime
2 measures/3 tbsp Bacardi white rum
5 measures/120ml/4 fl oz Coca-cola

1 Reserve a slice of lime for the garnish, then squeeze the juice directly into a highball glass half-filled with cracked ice, and then put the empty rind in too.

2 Add the rum, stir, and finally top up with ice-cold Coca-cola.

3 Garnish with the reserved slice of lime.

Nutritional information per portion: Energy 149kcal/622kJ; Protein 0g; Carbohydrate 13.1g, of which sugars 13.1g; Fat 0g, of which saturates 0g; Cholesterol 0mg; Calcium 7mg; Fibre 0g; Sodium 6mg; Alcohol 14.3g.

Continental

An old-fashioned mixture of rum and peppermint cordial was once a popular drink. This cocktail presents a more adventurous spin on that formula. The colour is an attractive shade of tawny, and the mint flavour is agreeably set off by the piercing note of lime.

MAKES 1 GLASS

1¹/₂ measures/6 tsp light rum
¹/₂ measure/2 tsp green crème
  de menthe
¹/₂ measure/2 tsp lime juice
sprig of mint, to garnish (optional)

1 Shake all the liquid ingredients well with ice in a cocktail shaker.

2 Strain into a cocktail glass.

3 If available, add a sprig of mint to the drink.

Nutritional information per portion: Energy 125kcal/524kJ; Protein 1.3g; Carbohydrate 10.1g, of which sugars 3.4g; Fat 0.2g, of which saturates 0g; Cholesterol 0mg; Calcium 14mg; Fibre 0.6g; Sodium 2mg; Alcohol 11.4g.

Hurricane

There are almost as many different recipes for a drink called Hurricane as there are cocktail books, but this particular one, with its exuberantly fruity character, is my favourite. With a medley of tropical flavours, as well as dark and white rum, the taste will transport you to a desert island.

MAKES 1 GLASS

1¹/₂ measures/6 tsp dark rum
1 measure/1¹/₂ tbsp white rum
1 measure/1¹/₂ tbsp lime juice
2 measures/3 tbsp passion fruit juice
1 measure/1¹/₂ tbsp pineapple juice
1 measure/1¹/₂ tbsp orange juice
¹/₂ measure/2 tsp blackcurrant syrup
  (from a can of fruit)
slice of pineapple, slice of orange and
  a cherry, to garnish

1 Shake all the liquid ingredients well with ice in a cocktail shaker.

2 Strain into a highball glass.

3 Garnish with slices of pineapple and orange, and a cherry.

Nutritional information per portion: Energy 183kcal/768kJ; Protein 0.4g; Carbohydrate 15.8g, of which sugars 15.6g; Fat 0.1g, of which saturates 0g; Cholesterol 0mg; Calcium 9mg; Fibre 0g; Sodium 10mg; Alcohol 17.4g.

Zombie

This legendary 1930s cocktail recipe was created at Don the Beachcomber restaurant in Hollywood. It was reportedly made as a hangover cure! It has everything but the kitchen sink in it, and yet it is still a harmonious (and dynamic) mixture.

MAKES 1 GLASS

1 measure/1 1/2 tbsp light rum
1/2 measure/2 tsp dark rum
1/2 measure/2 tsp white rum
1 measure/1 1/2 tbsp orange curaçao
1/4 measure/1 tsp Pernod
1 measure/1 1/2 tbsp lemon juice
1 measure/1 1/2 tbsp orange juice
1 measure/1 1/2 tbsp pineapple juice
1/2 measure/2 tsp papaya juice
1/4 measure/1 tsp grenadine
1/2 measure/2 tsp orgeat (almond syrup)
1/4 measure/1 tsp overproof rum
slice of pineapple, slice of lime and
    a cherry, to garnish

1 Blend all the liquid ingredients but the overproof rum with ice in a cocktail shaker.

2 Strain the drink into an ice-packed highball glass.

3 Sprinkle with overproof rum.

4 Garnish with a slice of pineapple, a slice of lime and a cherry.

Nutritional information per portion: Energy 286kcal/ 1196kJ; Protein 0.3g; Carbohydrate 21.1g, of which sugars 21.1g; Fat 0.1g, of which saturates 0g; Cholesterol 0mg; Calcium 7mg; Fibre 0.1g; Sodium 32mg; Alcohol 29.4g.

Piña Colada

This is one of the most popular cocktails worldwide, with a name meaning 'strained pineapple'. For a Caribbean touch, serve it in a hollowed-out pineapple shell, which also means that you can liquidize the flesh for the juice in the recipe. A bowl-shaped cocktail glass is the next best thing.

MAKES 1 GLASS

2 measures/3 tbsp white rum
2 measures/3 tbsp pineapple juice
1¹/₂ measures/6 tsp coconut cream
5ml/1 tsp caster (superfine) sugar
   (if freshly blended fruit is used)
slice of pineapple and a cherry,
   to garnish

1 Shake all the ingredients well with ice in a cocktail shaker.

2 Strain into a cocktail goblet.

3 Garnish with a slice of pineapple and a cherry.

BARTENDING KNOW-HOW
If you can't get hold of coconut cream, the equivalent quantity of any coconut liqueur such as Malibu may be used to good effect.

Nutritional information per portion: Energy 268kcal/ 1112kJ; Protein 1.4g; Carbohydrate 10.3g, of which sugars 10.3g; Fat 13.8g, of which saturates 11.9g; Cholesterol 0mg; Calcium 10mg; Fibre 0g; Sodium 10mg; Alcohol 14.3g.

Jamaican Black Coffee

There are any number of combinations of alcohol with hot brewed coffee, some more successful than others. This delicious version of black coffee is in fact only slightly alcoholic but gains extra allure from the inclusion of citrus fruits. The recipe serves eight.

MAKES 8 GLASSES

1 lemon and 2 oranges, finely sliced
1.5 litres/2½ pints black coffee
   (filter/cafetière brewed using
   55g/2oz coffee per 1 litre/
   1¾ pints water)
2 measures/3 tbsp light rum
85g/3oz caster (superfine) sugar

1 Place the lemon and orange slices in a pan, reserving eight lemon slices for the garnish. Add the coffee and heat.

2 When the mixture is about to boil, pour in the rum and sugar, stirring well until the sugar dissolves, then immediately remove from the heat.

3 While the coffee is still very hot, pour or ladle into heatproof glasses, and garnish with a fresh lemon slice.

Nutritional information per portion: Energy 465kcal/1962kJ; Protein 3.4g; Carbohydrate 93.3g, of which sugars 88.8g; Fat 0g, of which saturates 0g; Cholesterol 0mg; Calcium 90mg; Fibre 0g; Sodium 5mg; Alcohol 14.3g.

Passion Punch

Although it is not really a punch at all, the combination of passion fruit and grape juices in this recipe is a winning one. The acidity of the one is mitigated by the sweetness of the other, with the pineapple syrup adding a viscous texture to the drink.

MAKES 1 GLASS

1¹/₂ **measures/6 tsp light rum**
1 **measure/1¹/₂ tbsp red grape juice**
1 **measure/1¹/₂ tbsp passion fruit juice**
¹/₄ **measure/1 tsp pineapple syrup**
 (from a can)
piece of kumquat rind, to garnish

1 Shake all the ingredients well with ice in a cocktail shaker.

2 Strain into a rocks glass.

3 Garnish with a piece of kumquat rind, if you like.

Nutritional information per portion: Energy 111kcal/465kJ; Protein 0.2g; Carbohydrate 11.6g, of which sugars 11.6g; Fat 0g, of which saturates 0g; Cholesterol 0mg; Calcium 10mg; Fibre 0g; Sodium 25mg; Alcohol 9.6g.

Tequila Sunrise

This classic Mexican recipe of the 1930s takes its name from the way the grenadine – bright red pomegranate cordial – first sinks in the glass of orange juice and then rises to the surface. Add it too slowly and it will simply blend into the drink, turning it a scarlet colour.

MAKES 1 GLASS

2 measures/3 tbsp gold tequila
4 measures/6 tbsp freshly squeezed
    orange juice
1/2 measure/2 tsp grenadine
slice of orange and a cherry, to garnish (optional)

1 Half-fill a highball glass with crushed ice.

2 Pour in the tequila, then the orange juice, which must be freshly squeezed.

3 Quickly add the grenadine, pouring it down the back of a spoon held inside the glass so that it sinks to the bottom of the drink.

4 You could garnish the drink with a slice of orange and a cherry, if you like.

Nutritional information per portion: Energy 159kcal/661kJ; Protein 0.5g; Carbohydrate 11.2g, of which sugars 11.2g; Fat 0.1g, of which saturates 0g; Cholesterol 0mg; Calcium 10mg; Fibre 0.1g; Sodium 10mg; Alcohol 16.3g.

Tequila Sunset

This variation on the popular party drink (pictured right) can be mixed and chilled in a jug (pitcher), ready to pour into glasses, and finished at the last minute with the sweet addition of crème de cassis and honey. It is a stunning cocktail, which never fails to impress.

MAKES 1 GLASS

1 measure/1 1/2 tbsp gold tequila
5 measures/120ml/4fl oz lemon juice
1 measure/1 1/2 tbsp orange juice
15–30ml/1–2 tbsp clear honey
2/3 measure/1 tbsp crème de cassis

1 Pour the tequila, and lemon and orange juices into a well-chilled cocktail glass.

2 Using a swizzle-stick, mix the ingredients together well.

3 Trickle the honey into the centre of the drink. It will sink and create a layer at the bottom of the glass.

4 Add the crème de cassis, but do not stir. It will create a glowing layer above the honey at the bottom of the cocktail glass.

Nutritional information per portion: Energy 153kcal/644kJ; Protein 0.6g; Carbohydrate 21.2g, of which sugars 21.2g; Fat 0g, of which saturates 0g; Cholesterol 0mg; Calcium 13mg; Fibre 0.2g; Sodium 8mg; Alcohol 10g.

Margarita

With the Tequila Sunrise, Margarita (created in Tijuana in the late 1940s) is probably the best-known tequila cocktail of them all, and these days is a sight more popular. Its saltiness and sourness make it a great aperitif, and it is pleasingly strong too. Some recipes use lemon juice instead of lime, but lime juice sharpens its bite.

MAKES 1 GLASS

1$^{1}/_{2}$ measures/6 tsp silver tequila
$^{1}/_{2}$ measure/2 tsp Cointreau
juice of a lime
twist of cucumber rind or a half-slice
   of lime, to garnish

1 Rub the rim of a cocktail glass with a wedge of fresh lime and then dip it in fine salt.

2 Shake the tequila, Cointreau and lime juice with plenty of ice, then strain into the prepared glass.

3 Garnish with a twist of cucumber rind or a half-slice of lime.

Nutritional information per portion: Energy 95kcal/396kJ; Protein 0.1g; Carbohydrate 3.8g, of which sugars 3.8g; Fat 0g, of which saturates 0g; Cholesterol 0mg; Calcium 3mg; Fibre 0g; Sodium 2mg; Alcohol 11.4g.

Tequila Slammer

The Slammer, served in a shot glass, reflects something of the bravado with which tequila is traditionally drunk in Mexico. It is a drink in which one takes over the bartender's performance ethic for oneself, and it has recently, not surprisingly, become internationally practised among a certain age group.

MAKES 1 GLASS

1 measure/1¹/₂ tbsp silver or gold tequila
1 measure/1¹/₂ tbsp sparkling mixer
    (usually either lemonade or ginger ale,
    but can be sparkling wine)

1 Pour the two measures into a shot glass.

2 Cover with the palm of your hand (or a beer mat, if you don't fancy getting messy) and slam the glass down a couple of times on the bar counter or table.

3 The drink will then fizz wildly up, and you have something less than a second to get it to your mouth and down it in one.

Nutritional information per portion: Energy 53kcal/221kJ;
Protein 0g; Carbohydrate 0.9g, of which sugars 0.9g;
Fat 0g, of which saturates 0g; Cholesterol 0mg;
Calcium 0mg; Fibre 0g; Sodium 0mg; Alcohol 7.1g.

Iced Margarita

This smooth sorbet drink has all the punch of Mexico's renowned Margarita cocktail, but is also wonderfully refreshing on a hot day. This recipe makes two drinks.

MAKES 2 GLASSES

lemon and lime slices
2$^1/_2$ measures/3$^1/_2$ tbsp silver tequila
1$^1/_4$ measures/5$^1/_2$ tsp Cointreau
1$^1/_4$ measures/5$^1/_2$ tsp lime juice
6–8 small scoops lime sorbet
150ml/$^1/_4$ pint chilled lemonade
sprig of lemon balm, to garnish

1 Frost the rims of two large cocktail glasses with cut lime and caster (superfine) sugar.

2 Add lime and lemon slices to each.

3 Mix the tequila, Cointreau and lime juice in a jug (pitcher).

4 Scoop the sorbet into the glasses.

5 Pour an equal quantity of the drink into each glass. Top with lemonade and garnish with lemon balm.

Nutritional information per portion: Energy 250kcal/
1058kJ; Protein 1g; Carbohydrate 42.2g, of which
sugars 42.2g; Fat 0g, of which saturates 0g;
Cholesterol 0mg; Calcium 7mg; Fibre 0g; Sodium 24mg;
Alcohol 12.7g.

Mango and Peach Margarita

Adding puréed fruit to the classic tequila mixture alters the consistency to a thicker, dense drink. This recipe serves four and should be served in cocktail glasses.

MAKES 4 GLASSES

2 mangoes, peeled and sliced
3 peaches, peeled and sliced
5 measures/120ml/4fl oz silver tequila
2½ measures/3½ tbsp Cointreau
2½ measures/3½ tbsp lime juice

1 Reserve eight slices of mango for the garnish, then blend the remaining mango and peach slices in a liquidizer until a smooth paste is obtained.

2 Add the tequila, Cointreau and lime juice, blend for a few seconds more, then add the ice.

3 Blend again until the drink has the consistency of a milkshake.

4 Pour into pre-chilled cocktail glasses and garnish with the reserved slices of mango.

Nutritional information per portion: Energy 176kcal/742kJ; Protein 1.3g; Carbohydrate 19.7g, of which sugars 19.5g; Fat 0.2g, of which saturates 0.1g; Cholesterol 0mg; Calcium 15mg; Fibre 3.1g; Sodium 3mg; Alcohol 13.7g.

Sangrita

Sipping sangrita and tequila alternately is a taste sensation not to be missed, the warm flavours of the first balancing the strength of the second. The drinks are often served with antojitos (nibbles) as an appetizer. This recipe serves eight.

MAKES 8 GLASSES

450g/1lb ripe tomatoes, or one
    400g/14oz can chopped tomatoes
1 small onion, finely chopped
2 small fresh green chillies, seeded
    and chopped
120ml/4fl oz freshly squeezed orange juice
juice of 3 limes
2.5ml/$\frac{1}{2}$ tsp caster (superfine) sugar
pinch of salt
8 measures/12 tbsp gold or aged tequila

1 Cut a large cross in the base of each tomato. Place in a heatproof bowl and pour over boiling water to cover. Leave for 3 minutes. Remove the tomatoes and plunge them into cold water. Remove the skins, then cut the tomatoes in half and scoop out the seeds with a spoon.

2 Chop the tomato flesh. Put it in a food processor. Add the onion, chillies, orange juice, lime juice, sugar and salt. Process until smooth, then pour into a jug (pitcher). Chill for an hour.

3 Offer each drinker a separate shot glass of neat tequila as well. The drinks are sipped alternately.

Nutritional information per portion: Energy 75kcal/314kJ; Protein 0.7g; Carbohydrate 4g, of which sugars 3.9g; Fat 0.2g, of which saturates 0.1g; Cholesterol 0mg; Calcium 9mg; Fibre 0.7g; Sodium 7mg; Alcohol 7.9g.

Piñata

An odd name this, as you might think it contained pineapple, but no – banana and lime are the
fruit flavours in this cocktail. It is, nonetheless, quite delicious in its simplicity of fruity flavours.
Serve this drink in a cocktail glass, garnished with a twist of lime rind.

MAKES 1 GLASS

1¹/₂ measures/6 tsp gold tequila
1 measure/1¹/₂ tbsp crème de banane
1 measure/1¹/₂ tbsp lime juice
lime rind, to garnish

1 Shake all the liquid ingredients
well with ice in a cocktail shaker.

2 Strain into a cocktail glass.

3 Twist the lime rind and dangle it
in the drink to garnish.

BARTENDING KNOW-HOW

Gold tequila is richer and more complex
than the basic silver tequila, and it is
aged in wooden casks.

Nutritional information per portion: Energy 134kcal/558kJ;
Protein 0.1g; Carbohydrate 7.7g, of which sugars 7.7g;
Fat 0g, of which saturates 0g; Cholesterol 0mg;
Calcium 3mg; Fibre 0g; Sodium 3mg; Alcohol 14.9g.

Bloody Maria

A close cousin of the original vodka-based Bloody Mary, this simple cocktail consists of tequila and tomato juice mixed together with spicy seasonings. The quantities here make two drinks, just in case that hangover is particularly persistent, or you have a fellow sufferer.

MAKES 2 GLASSES

250ml/8fl oz tomato juice, chilled
2 measures/3 tbsp silver tequila
5ml/1 tsp Worcestershire sauce
few drops Tabasco
juice of half a lemon
pinch celery salt
salt and freshly ground black pepper
2 celery sticks, to garnish

1 Pour the chilled tomato juice into a large jug (pitcher) and stir in the tequila.

2 Add the Worcestershire sauce and stir the mixture well.

3 Add a few drops of Tabasco and the lemon juice. Taste and season with celery salt, salt and pepper.

4 Serve over ice cubes in highball glasses, with celery sticks standing in the drink for stirring it.

BARTENDING KNOW-HOW
The tequila naturally makes its presence felt in this mixture more obviously than vodka does.

Nutritional information per portion: Energy 140kcal/590kJ; Protein 2.1g; Carbohydrate 8.7g, of which sugars 8.6g; Fat 0g, of which saturates 0g; Cholesterol 0mg; Calcium 36mg; Fibre 1.5g; Sodium 635mg; Alcohol 14.3g.

Pineapple Tequila

Flavours such as almond and quince have been added to silver tequila for some time. Many bars have developed unique flavours by combining ingredients such as chillies with tequila, and leaving them to infuse. The method below will make a smooth, fruity drink to serve six.

MAKES 6 GLASSES

1 large pineapple, cut into small chunks
50g/2oz soft dark brown sugar
1 litre/1³/₄ pints silver tequila
1 vanilla pod (bean)

1 Rinse a 2 litre/3¹/₂ pint wide-necked bottle. Sterilize it by placing it in an oven, turning on the oven and setting it at 110°C/225°F/Gas ¹/₄. After 20 minutes, remove the bottle and allow to cool completely.

2 Put the pineapple into the bottle. Mix the sugar and tequila in a jug (pitcher) until the sugar dissolves, then pour into the bottle. Split the vanilla pod. Add it to the bottle.

3 Gently agitate the bottle a few times each day to stir the contents. Allow the tequila to stand for at least a week before drinking with ice.

BARTENDING KNOW-HOW
When the tequila is gone, serve the pineapple with ice cream, or warm with butter and cinnamon, and cream.

Nutritional information per portion: Energy 458kcal/
1907kJ; Protein 0.6g; Carbohydrate 22.2g, of which
sugars 22.2g; Fat 0.3g, of which saturates 0g;
Cholesterol 0mg; Calcium 29mg; Fibre 1.6g;
Sodium 3mg; Alcohol 5.2g.

Whisky and Brandy

It is perhaps whisky that is the trickiest base

ingredient to use in cocktails. Rich, woody

American whiskeys, such as bourbon and rye,

and fruity Canadian whisky, are better in

this respect than Scotch, which, with its

iodiney pungency, is best enjoyed on its own.

Brandy has long held a certain status and

all brandies are good mixers in cocktails.

Although you won't want to use your best

cognac, don't use the cheapest grades either.

Rusty Nail

A short, sharp drink, this is another classic half-and-half recipe, and one that still manages to do perfect justice to both ingredients – Scotch and Drambuie. The key to this drink's superb flavour lies in its simplicity – serve it ungarnished in a tumbler with ice, and enjoy.

MAKES 1 GLASS

1¹/₂ **measures/6 tsp Scotch**
1¹/₂ **measures/6 tsp Drambuie**

1 Pour both ingredients over crushed ice in a rocks glass or whisky tumbler.

2 Stir gently. No garnish is necessary. Some prefer to leave the ice cubes whole so as not to dilute the drink too much. It should be drunk quickly.

BARTENDING KNOW-HOW
A Rusty Nail is really the Drambuie cocktail. Attempts to make this fine Scottish liqueur blend with anything other than Scotch always seem to come to grief. It genuinely seems to be too good to mix.

Nutritional information per portion: Energy 161kcal/670kJ; Protein 0g; Carbohydrate 7.3g, of which sugars 7.3g; Fat 0g, of which saturates 0g; Cholesterol 0mg; Calcium 0mg; Fibre 0g; Sodium 2mg; Alcohol 19g.

Whisky Mac

The classic cold remedy is half-and-half good Scotch and green ginger wine (preferably Crabbie's). These days, it is generally served over ice in a rocks glass, but traditionally it was taken straight up. Whether it gets rid of a cold is open to doubt, but it certainly makes you feel better.

MAKES 1 GLASS

1¹/₂ **measures/6 tsp Scotch**
1¹/₂ **measures/6 tsp green ginger wine**

1 Pour the Scotch and green ginger wine into a rocks glass.

2 Stir gently. No garnish is necessary. Serve this drink on ice, if you prefer.

Nutritional information per portion: Energy 109kcal/454kJ;
Protein 0g; Carbohydrate 7.4g, of which sugars 7.4g;
Fat 0g, of which saturates 0g; Cholesterol 0mg;
Calcium 1mg; Fibre 0g; Sodium 3mg; Alcohol 11.6g.

Whisky Sour

American whiskeys (spelt with an 'e') are best for this type of preparation. Some people like to add a brief squirt of soda to the drink. If you find this formula a little too sour, you could always add a bit more sugar, but this is the way I like it. Serve it simply over ice.

MAKES 1 GLASS

juice of 1/2 lemon
5ml/1 tsp caster (superfine) sugar
1 measure/11/2 tbsp whisky
slice of lemon, to garnish

1 Mix the lemon juice with the caster sugar in a small tumbler with two or three cubes of ice.

2 When the sugar is dissolved, add a generous measure of whisky and stir again.

3 Thread a slice of lemon on to a cocktail stick (toothpick), to garnish.

Nutritional information per portion: Energy 67kcal/282kJ; Protein 0.1g; Carbohydrate 4.6g, of which sugars 4.6g; Fat 0g, of which saturates 0g; Cholesterol 0mg; Calcium 4mg; Fibre 0g; Sodium 0mg; Alcohol 7.2g.

Perfect Manhattan

When making Manhattans it's a matter of preference whether you use sweet vermouth, dry vermouth or a mixture of the two. Both of the former require a dash of Angostura bitters. The last, given here, is such a harmoniously balanced mixture that it doesn't need it.

MAKES 1 GLASS

2 measures/3 tbsp rye whiskey
1/4 measure/1 tsp dry vermouth
1/4 measure/1 tsp sweet red vermouth
small strip of lemon rind and a
    maraschino cherry, to garnish

1 Pour the whiskey and vermouths into a bar glass half-full of ice.

2 Stir well for 30 seconds to mix and chill.

3 Strain on the rocks or straight up into a chilled cocktail glass.

4 Pare away a small strip of lemon rind. Tie it into a knot to help release the oils from the rind, then drop it into the cocktail.

5 Add the cherry with its stalk left intact. As any Manhattan drinker will tell you, the cherry is essential.

Nutritional information per portion: Energy 113kcal/468kJ;
Protein 0g; Carbohydrate 0.9g, of which sugars 0.9g;
Fat 0g, of which saturates 0g; Cholesterol 0mg;
Calcium 1mg; Fibre 0g; Sodium 2mg; Alcohol 15.6g.

Gall Bracer

Short and smart, this drink is served on the rocks in a tumbler, or in a long-stemmed glass with a maraschino cherry. It all depends on the drinker and the occasion.

MAKES 1 GLASS

2 dashes of Angostura bitters
2 dashes of grenadine
2 measures/3 tbsp bourbon
    or rye whiskey
lemon rind
maraschino cherry,
    to garnish (optional)

1 Half-fill a bar glass with ice cubes. Add the Angostura bitters, grenadine and whiskey, and stir well to chill.

2 Place some ice in a small tumbler and pour the cocktail over it. Squeeze lemon rind over the top and then discard. Garnish with a cherry, if desired. For a longer drink, finish with soda or sparkling mineral water.

Nutritional information per portion: Energy 113kcal/469kJ; Protein 0g; Carbohydrate 1.6g, of which sugars 1.6g; Fat 0g, of which saturates 0g; Cholesterol 0mg; Calcium 0mg; Fibre 0g; Sodium 1mg; Alcohol 15.3g.

Blizzard

The trick with this drink is to shake it for longer than normal with masses of ice until the mixture is frosty-looking. That incidentally goes some way to disguise the high proportion of bourbon in it.

MAKES 1 GLASS

3 measures/4¹/₂ tbsp bourbon
1 measure/1¹/₂ tbsp cranberry juice
²/₃ measure/1 tbsp lemon juice
30ml/2 tbsp sugar syrup
slice of lemon and cranberries, to garnish

1 Shake all the liquid ingredients extremely well in a cocktail shaker with plenty of large ice cubes.

2 Pour the mixture, unstrained, into a chilled highball glass. Garnish with a slice of lemon and a couple of cranberries.

Nutritional information per portion: Energy 153kcal/634kJ; Protein 0g; Carbohydrate 2.2g, of which sugars 2.2g; Fat 0g, of which saturates 0g; Cholesterol 0mg; Calcium 2mg; Fibre 0g; Sodium 0mg; Alcohol 20.5g.

Artists' Special

This drink (pictured right) is so-named because it was invented at the Artists' Club in the rue Pigalle, Paris, in the 1920s. The red ingredient was originally redcurrant syrup, but grenadine can be used to perfectly good effect instead.

MAKES 1 GLASS

1 measure/1¹/2 tbsp Scotch
1 measure/1¹/2 tbsp sweet brown sherry
1/2 measure/2 tsp lemon juice
1/2 measure/2 tsp grenadine
half-slice of lemon, to garnish

1 Shake all the liquid ingredients well with ice in a cocktail shaker.

2 Strain into a cocktail glass. Add a half-slice of lemon, to garnish.

Nutritional information per portion: Energy 107kcal/448kJ; Protein 0.1g; Carbohydrate 5g, of which sugars 5g; Fat 0g, of which saturates 0g; Cholesterol 0mg; Calcium 3mg; Fibre 0g; Sodium 4mg; Alcohol 12.6g.

Pleasant Dreams

The mixture of blackberry and peach flavours in this fruity treatment for bourbon would make a very comforting, sweet-tasting nightcap – so long as you confine yourself to just the one, that is.

MAKES 1 GLASS

1¹/2 measures/6 tsp bourbon
³/4 measure/3 tsp crème de mûre
¹/4 measure/1 tsp peach schnapps

1 Shake the bourbon, crème de mûre and peach schnapps well with ice in a cocktail shaker.

2 Pour without straining into a chilled rocks glass.

Nutritional information per portion: Energy 119kcal/496kJ; Protein 0g; Carbohydrate 6.6g, of which sugars 6.6g; Fat 0g, of which saturates 0g; Cholesterol 0mg; Calcium 1mg; Fibre 0g; Sodium 2mg; Alcohol 13.4g.

Kentucky Kernel

The geographical reference of this drink indicates that it's a bourbon cocktail, and the second half of the name refers to the apricot kernels from which its other alcoholic ingredient is made. The grapefruit juice brings it all into focus.

MAKES 1 GLASS

1¹/₂ **measures/6 tsp bourbon**
¹/₂ **measure/2 tsp apricot brandy**
1 **measure/1¹/₂ tbsp grapefruit juice**
¹/₄ **measure/1 tsp grenadine**

1 Shake all the ingredients well with ice in a cocktail shaker.

2 Pour the drink – ice and all – into a rocks glass.

Nutritional information per portion: Energy 113kcal/469kJ;
Protein 0.1g; Carbohydrate 6.8g, of which sugars 6.8g;
Fat 0g, of which saturates 0g; Cholesterol 0mg;
Calcium 3mg; Fibre 0g; Sodium 2mg; Alcohol 12.4g.

Rocky Mountain

Here is another one of those cocktails that calls for three specific brands of spirits to be used – and it wouldn't be quite the same if you made it using substitutes. Its light, delicately herbal tinge is very attractive. Serve it on ice in a chilled rocks glass.

MAKES 1 GLASS

1¹/₂ measures/6 tsp Canadian Club
¹/₂ measure/2 tsp Glayva
¹/₄ measure/1 tsp Punt e Mes

1 Shake all the ingredients well with ice in a cocktail shaker.

2 Pour the cocktail, without straining, into a chilled rocks glass.

BARTENDING KNOW-HOW
The Italian aperitif Punt e Mes, created in Turin in 1870, contains around four dozen herbs and spices on a white wine base. In Italy, it is traditionally accompanied by a piece of strong, dark (bittersweet) chocolate.

Nutritional information per portion: Energy 98kcal/408kJ; Protein 0g; Carbohydrate 3.4g, of which sugars 3.4g; Fat 0g, of which saturates 0g; Cholesterol 0mg; Calcium 1mg; Fibre 0g; Sodium 2mg; Alcohol 12.1g.

Duck Soup

A fruity preparation in which bourbon is given the treatment more normally accorded to rum. It works well, though, showing what a versatile drink American whiskey is.

MAKES 1 GLASS

2 measures/3 tbsp bourbon
¹/₂ measure/2 tsp apricot brandy
³/₄ measure/3 tsp lemon juice
³/₄ measure/3 tsp pineapple juice
5ml/1 tsp caster (superfine) sugar
slice of lemon and a cherry, to garnish

1 Shake the bourbon, apricot brandy, lemon juice, pineapple juice and caster sugar well with ice in a cocktail shaker.

2 Strain into a rocks glass that is half-filled with cracked ice.

3 Garnish with a slice of lemon and a cherry.

BARTENDING KNOW-HOW
Bourbon can technically be made anywhere in the United States, as its name isn't a geographical designation. Its traditional home state, however, is Kentucky, which is the only one allowed to put its name on the label. Tennessee whiskey may not be called Tennessee bourbon because when the labelling laws were drawn up in the 19th century, Kentucky had more senators than its southern neighbour.

Nutritional information per portion: Energy 148kcal/619kJ; Protein 0.1g; Carbohydrate 9.3g, of which sugars 9.3g; Fat 0g, of which saturates 0g; Cholesterol 0mg; Calcium 4mg; Fibre 0g; Sodium 2mg; Alcohol 16.1g.

Pamplemousse

The name is the French word for 'grapefruit', and so it's not hard to work out what the principal flavour of this charming cocktail should be.

MAKES 1 GLASS

1¹/₂ measures/6 tsp Canadian whisky
¹/₂ measure/2 tsp Southern Comfort
2 measures/3 tbsp grapefruit juice
¹/₄ measure/1 tsp pineapple syrup
short twist of grapefruit rind and a
    cocktail cherry, to garnish

1 Shake all the liquid ingredients well with ice in a cocktail shaker.

2 Strain into a rocks glass half-filled with cracked ice.

3 Add the grapefruit rind and a cocktail cherry.

BARTENDING KNOW-HOW
Both Canadian whisky and Southern Comfort have a pronounced fruity flavour, the latter derived at least partly from the use of peaches. They work particularly well in fruity mixtures such as this one.

Nutritional information per portion: Energy 118kcal/494kJ; Protein 0.2g; Carbohydrate 7.7g, of which sugars 7.7g; Fat 0g, of which saturates 0g; Cholesterol 0mg; Calcium 7mg; Fibre 0g; Sodium 4mg; Alcohol 12.7g.

Highland Morning

Despite the name of this cocktail (pictured right) it might be wiser to drink one of these a little later in the day.

MAKES 1 GLASS

1 measure/1¹/₂ tbsp Scotch
³/₄ measure/3 tsp Cointreau
3 measures/4¹/₂ tbsp grapefruit juice
twist of grapefruit rind and a half-slice of orange, to garnish (optional)

1 Shake all the liquid ingredients well with ice in a cocktail shaker.

2 Pour (unstrained if you really are having it in the morning) into a chilled rocks glass.

3 The drink could be garnished with a twist of grapefruit rind and perhaps a half-slice of orange to reflect the presence of Cointreau in the mix, if you like.

Nutritional information per portion: Energy 119kcal/498kJ; Protein 0.3g; Carbohydrate 9.3g, of which sugars 9.3g; Fat 0.1g, of which saturates 0g; Cholesterol 0mg; Calcium 9mg; Fibre 0g; Sodium 6mg; Alcohol 11.9g.

Loch Ness

Named after the famous monster claimed to inhabit Loch Ness, this Scottish cocktail is a tough cookie. It dates from the 1920s.

MAKES 1 GLASS

1¹/₂ measures/6 tsp Scotch
1 measure/1¹/₂ tbsp Pernod
¹/₄ measure/1 tsp sweet red vermouth

1 Shake all the ingredients with ice in a cocktail shaker.

2 Pour without straining into a chilled rocks glass or Old-fashioned glass. Do not garnish.

Nutritional information per portion: Energy 145kcal/603kJ; Protein 0g; Carbohydrate 6.3g, of which sugars 6.3g; Fat 0g, of which saturates 0g; Cholesterol 0mg; Calcium 0mg; Fibre 0g; Sodium 3mg; Alcohol 17.3g.

Jack Frost

The Jack in the name refers to the ever-popular Tennessee whiskey brand, Jack Daniel's, so that is the type that should be used. This is an exotic and highly appealing cocktail, with tropical flavours of banana, passion fruit and pineapple.

MAKES 1 GLASS

1 measure/1¹/₂ tbsp Jack Daniel's
³/₄ measure/3 tsp dry vermouth
¹/₃ measure/1¹/₂ tsp crème de banane
1 measure/1¹/₂ tbsp passion fruit juice
¹/₃ measure/1¹/₂ tsp pineapple juice
slice of lemon and chunk of pineapple,
    to garnish (optional)

1 Shake all the liquid ingredients well with ice in a cocktail shaker.

2 Strain into a large cocktail glass that has been half-filled with crushed ice.

3 The drink could be garnished with a slice of lemon on a stick with a chunk of juicy, ripe pineapple, if you like.

Nutritional information per portion: Energy 98kcal/409kJ;
Protein 0.1g; Carbohydrate 6g, of which sugars 6g;
Fat 0g, of which saturates 0g; Cholesterol 0mg;
Calcium 4mg; Fibre 0g; Sodium 5mg; Alcohol 10.7g.

Paddy

Another traditional one, this was originally made with the Irish whiskey brand of the same name. In the 1920s, it had equal quantities of whiskey and vermouth and slightly less Angostura, which made for a sweeter result. This is today's drier and more sophisticated formula.

MAKES 1 GLASS

1¹/₂ **measures/6 tsp Irish whiskey**
³/₄ **measure/3 tsp sweet red vermouth**
3 dashes Angostura bitters
half-slice of lemon, to garnish

1 Shake all the liquid ingredients well with ice in a cocktail shaker.

2 Strain into a chilled cocktail glass.

3 Garnish with a half-slice of lemon.

Nutritional information per portion: Energy 89kcal/370kJ; Protein 0g; Carbohydrate 2.4g, of which sugars 2.4g; Fat 0g, of which saturates 0g; Cholesterol 0mg; Calcium 1mg; Fibre 0g; Sodium 4mg; Alcohol 11.4g.

Coffee Egg-nog

This is a rather special coffee drink, particularly suitable for daytime summer holiday festivities. The recipe serves six to eight people.

MAKES 6–8 GLASSES

8 eggs, separated
225g/8oz sugar
250ml/8fl oz cold strong coffee
  (espresso strength or filter/cafetière
  brewed at 75g/3oz coffee per
  1 litre/1³/₄ pints water)
220ml/7¹/₂fl oz Scotch or bourbon
220ml/7¹/₂fl oz double (heavy) cream
120ml/4fl oz whipped cream
ground nutmeg, to garnish

1 Thoroughly beat the egg yolks, then add the sugar, mixing well.

2 Heat gently in a pan over a low heat, stirring with a wooden spoon.

3 Allow to cool a few minutes, stir in the coffee and whisky, and then slowly add the cream, stirring well.

4 Beat the egg whites until stiff and stir into the egg-nog, mixing well. Pour into small round cups, top each with a small dollop of whipped cream and sprinkle nutmeg on top.

Nutritional information per portion: Energy 440kcal/1831kJ; Protein 7.2g; Carbohydrate 30.4g, of which sugars 30.3g; Fat 26.4g, of which saturates 14.5g; Cholesterol 244mg; Calcium 67mg; Fibre 0g; Sodium 82mg; Alcohol 8.7g.

Irish Chocolate Velvet

This is a luxurious creamy hot chocolate drink, with just a touch of alcohol to fortify it. It would be the perfect antidote to a winter morning spent working outdoors. The recipe serves four.

MAKES 4 GLASSES

250ml/8fl oz double (heavy) cream
400ml/14fl oz milk
115g/4oz milk chocolate, chopped
   into small pieces
30ml/2 tbsp (unsweetened)
   cocoa powder
60ml/4 tbsp Irish whiskey
whipped cream, for topping
milk chocolate curls, to garnish

1 Whip half the cream in a bowl until it is thick enough to hold its shape.

2 Place the milk and chocolate in a pan and heat gently, stirring, until the chocolate has melted. Whisk in the cocoa, then bring to the boil. Remove from the heat and stir in the remaining cream and the Irish whiskey.

3 Pour quickly into four warmed heatproof mugs or glasses and top each serving with a generous spoonful of the whipped cream, finishing with a garnish of milk chocolate curls.

Nutritional information per portion: Energy 562kcal/2332kJ; Protein 8g; Carbohydrate 23g, of which sugars 22.1g; Fat 45.7g, of which saturates 28.2g; Cholesterol 98mg; Calcium 224mg; Fibre 1.1g; Sodium 152mg; Alcohol 8.1g.

Memphis Belle

One of the earliest cocktail recipes to use Southern Comfort, this may look an unlikely idea, in that it blends a whiskey-based liqueur with brandy, but in its dry, sharply sour way, it works.

MAKES 1 GLASS

1¹/₂ **measures/6 tsp cognac**
³/₄ **measure/3 tsp Southern Comfort**
¹/₂ **measure/2 tsp lemon juice**
¹/₄ **measure/1 tsp orange bitters**
   (or curaçao)
twist of lemon, to garnish

1 Shake all the liquid ingredients well with ice in a cocktail shaker.

2 Strain into a chilled cocktail glass.

3 Garnish with a twist of lemon.

Nutritional information per portion: Energy 115kcal/477kJ; Protein 0g; Carbohydrate 3.9g, of which sugars 3.9g; Fat 0g, of which saturates 0g; Cholesterol 0mg; Calcium 1mg; Fibre 0g; Sodium 1mg; Alcohol 14.3g.

Via Veneto

Named after the street in Rome that was once a scene of bohemian glamour, this cocktail contains the Italian elderberry-flavoured liqueur Sambuca Romana.

MAKES 1 GLASS

1¹/₂ **measures/6 tsp cognac**
¹/₂ **measure/2 tsp Sambuca**
¹/₂ **measure/2 tsp lemon juice**
¹/₄ **measure/1 tsp sugar syrup**
¹/₂ **egg white**
slice of lemon, to garnish

1 Shake all the liquid ingredients well with ice in a cocktail shaker.

2 Strain into a chilled rocks glass.

3 Garnish with a slice of lemon.

Nutritional information per portion: Energy 78kcal/327kJ;
Protein 1.5g; Carbohydrate 4.2g, of which sugars 4.2g;
Fat 0g, of which saturates 0g; Cholesterol 0mg;
Calcium 3mg; Fibre 0g; Sodium 31mg; Alcohol 12g.

Savoy Hotel

It's a short step from London's Savoy Theatre to the American Bar in the hotel itself, where this cocktail was created. It's a pousse-café or layered drink that requires a steady hand.

MAKES 1 GLASS

1 measure/1¹/₂ tbsp brown crème
 de cacao
1 measure/1¹/₂ tbsp Bénédictine
1 measure/1¹/₂ tbsp cognac

1 Carefully pour each of the ingredients, in the order given in the ingredients, over the back of a spoon into a liqueur glass or sherry schooner to create a multi-layered drink.

2 Serve immediately, while the effect is intact.

Nutritional information per portion: Energy 191kcal/798kJ; Protein 0g; Carbohydrate 11g, of which sugars 11g; Fat 0g, of which saturates 0g; Cholesterol 0mg; Calcium 0mg; Fibre 0g; Sodium 3mg; Alcohol 21.4g.

Cranberry Kiss

In this delicious, full-flavoured cocktail, the tang of cranberry and pink grapefruit juices is balanced by the toffeeish sweetness of Marsala.

MAKES 1 GLASS

redcurrants, to garnish
1 egg white, lightly beaten, and
    15ml/1 tbsp caster (superfine)
    sugar, to garnish
1 measure/1^1/$_2$ tbsp cognac
2 measures/3 tbsp cranberry juice
2 measures/3 tbsp pink grapefruit juice
2 measures/3 tbsp Marsala dolce

1 For the garnish, lightly brush the redcurrants with the egg white. Shake sugar over them to cover with a frosting. Set aside to dry.

2 Shake the brandy and cranberry and grapefruit juices with ice in a cocktail shaker.

3 Strain into a well-chilled glass.

4 Tilt the glass slightly then slowly pour in the Marsala down the side.

5 Garnish with the redcurrants.

Nutritional information per portion: Energy 152kcal/637kJ;
Protein 3.4g; Carbohydrate 10.6g, of which sugars 10.6g;
Fat 0.1g, of which saturates 0g; Cholesterol 0mg;
Calcium 17mg; Fibre 0g; Sodium 73mg; Alcohol 14.2g.

Lake Como

The geographical reference recalls the origins of the excellent Italian liqueur used in this recipe. You'll never want another Black Russian after tasting this.

MAKES 1 GLASS

1¹/₂ measures/6 tsp cognac
³/₄ measure/3 tsp Tuaca
twist of lemon rind, to garnish

1 Mix the cognac and Tuaca well with ice in a large glass.

2 Strain into an old-fashioned or small rocks glass.

3 Squeeze a twist of lemon rind over the drink and then drop it into the glass. This is one for drinking quickly and confidently.

Nutritional information per portion: Energy 106kcal/441kJ; Protein 0g; Carbohydrate 4.9g, of which sugars 4.9g; Fat 0g, of which saturates 0g; Cholesterol 0mg; Calcium 1mg; Fibre 0g; Sodium 2mg; Alcohol 12.4g.

Brandy Melba

*As might be expected, this is a very fruity cocktail that could almost pass as a sort of dessert.
It uses the combination of peach and raspberry in the classic Peach Melba dessert.*

MAKES 1 GLASS

1¹/₂ **measures/6 tsp cognac**
¹/₂ **measure/2 tsp peach schnapps**
¹/₄ **measure/1 tsp crème de framboise**
¹/₂ **measure/2 tsp lemon juice**
¹/₄ **measure/1 tsp orange bitters**
    (or curaçao)
slice of ripe peach and a raspberry,
    to garnish

1 Shake all the liquid ingredients
well with ice in a cocktail shaker.

2 Strain into a chilled cocktail glass.

3 Garnish with a slice of ripe peach
and a raspberry.

Nutritional information per portion: Energy 103kcal/427kJ;
Protein 0g; Carbohydrate 4.9g, of which sugars 4.9g;
Fat 0g, of which saturates 0g; Cholesterol 0mg;
Calcium 1mg; Fibre 0g; Sodium 2mg; Alcohol 9g.

Brandy Fix

A Fix is a mixture of spirit with lemon juice, sweetening and in this case another alcohol flavour, with the shell of the lemon and a pile of ice left in the drink for good measure.

MAKES 1 GLASS

5ml/1 tsp sugar
juice and rind of half a lemon
1¹/₂ measures/6 tsp cognac
³/₄ measure/3 tsp cherry brandy

1 Dissolve the sugar in a little water in the bottom of a small tumbler, then fill it with crushed ice.

2 Add the lemon juice, cognac and cherry brandy, and stir well.

3 Drop in the squeezed lemon rind.

Nutritional information per portion: Energy 125kcal/521kJ; Protein 0g; Carbohydrate 10.1g, of which sugars 10.1g; Fat 0g, of which saturates 0g; Cholesterol 0mg; Calcium 3mg; Fibre 0g; Sodium 0mg; Alcohol 12.4g.

B & B

The traditional mix of this world-famous cocktail is half-and-half Bénédictine and good brandy (cognac for preference), stirred not shaken, and not usually iced. No garnish is needed.

MAKES 1 GLASS

1¹/₂ **measures/6 tsp cognac**
1¹/₂ **measures/6 tsp Bénédictine**

1 Pour the two ingredients into a balloon glass, cognac first.

2 Either stir the drink gently using a stirrer, or simply swirl the glass in your hand.

Nutritional information per portion: Energy 121kcal/502kJ;
Protein 0g; Carbohydrate 5.5g, of which sugars 5.5g;
Fat 0g, of which saturates 0g; Cholesterol 0mg;
Calcium 0mg; Fibre 0g; Sodium 1mg; Alcohol 14.3g.

Champarelle

Dating from the late 19th century, this is one of the oldest recipes for the layered drink. It helps if the ingredients and the glass are pre-chilled, as they are not mixed and you can't put ice in the drink.

MAKES 1 GLASS

$^1/_2$ **measure/2 tsp orange curaçao**
$^1/_2$ **measure/2 tsp yellow Chartreuse**
$^1/_2$ **measure/2 tsp anisette**
$^1/_2$ **measure/2 tsp cognac**

1 Carefully pour the orange curaçao over the back of a large spoon into a liqueur glass or sherry schooner.

2 Using a clean spoon, repeat with the yellow Chartreuse, then the anisette, and finally the cognac. Use a clean spoon for each ingredient and ensure that they remain in separate layers.

Nutritional information per portion: Energy 113kcal/472kJ; Protein 0g; Carbohydrate 6.3g, of which sugars 6.3g; Fat 0g, of which saturates 0g; Cholesterol 0mg; Calcium 1mg; Fibre 0g; Sodium 2mg; Alcohol 12.9g.

Last Goodbye

The flavours of cherry brandy and Cointreau are seen as being particularly compatible with cognac, and this is another appealing mixture.

MAKES 1 GLASS

1 measure/1¹⁄₂ tbsp cognac
³⁄₄ measure/3 tsp cherry brandy
¹⁄₄ measure/1 tsp Cointreau
¹⁄₂ measure/2 tsp lime juice
¹⁄₄ measure/1 tsp grenadine
slice of lime and a cherry,
    to garnish (optional)

1 Shake all the liquid ingredients well with ice in a cocktail shaker.

2 Strain into a balloon glass.

3 Garnish with a lime slice and a cherry, if you like.

Nutritional information per portion: Energy 120kcal/499kJ;
Protein 0g; Carbohydrate 7.3g, of which sugars 7.3g;
Fat 0g, of which saturates 0g; Cholesterol 0mg;
Calcium 0mg; Fibre 0g; Sodium 1mg; Alcohol 13.1g.

Port Side

The purply-red colour of this very sophisticated short drink looks extremely fetching sinking through a snowdrift of crushed ice.

MAKES 1 GLASS

1¹/₂ measures/6 tsp cognac
¹/₂ measure/2 tsp ruby port
¹/₂ measure/2 tsp crème de mûre
blackberry, to garnish (optional)

1 Stir all the liquid ingredients with ice in a jug (pitcher).

2 Strain into a rocks glass half-filled with crushed ice.

3 Garnish with a blackberry, if you happen to have one to hand.

Nutritional information per portion: Energy 109kcal/451kJ; Protein 0g; Carbohydrate 4.5g, of which sugars 4.5g; Fat 0g, of which saturates 0g; Cholesterol 0mg; Calcium 1mg; Fibre 0g; Sodium 2mg; Alcohol 13.1g.

Apple Sour

For those who don't fancy swallowing raw egg, this drink can be made without the egg white.
Applejack or apple schnapps also work well in place of the calvados.

MAKES 1 GLASS

1 measure/1¹/₂ tbsp cognac
1 measure/1¹/₂ tbsp calvados
²/₃ measure/1 tbsp lemon juice
5ml/1 tsp sugar
dash Angostura bitters
1 egg white
slice each of red and green apple,
   dipped in lemon juice, to garnish

1 Shake the cognac, calvados,
lemon juice, sugar, Angostura bitters
and egg white well with ice in a
cocktail shaker.

2 Strain into a tumbler half-filled
with cracked ice.

3 Garnish the drink with slices of
red and green apple dipped in
lemon juice.

Nutritional information per portion: Energy 128kcal/534kJ;
Protein 2.9g; Carbohydrate 4.4g, of which sugars 4.4g;
Fat 0g, of which saturates 0g; Cholesterol 0mg;
Calcium 5mg; Fibre 0g; Sodium 61mg; Alcohol 14.3g.

Never on Sunday

This recipe uses Metaxa, the caramelly Greek brandy, together with its compatriot, aniseedy ouzo, for a thoroughly Mediterranean experience.

MAKES 1 GLASS

1 measure/1¹/₂ tbsp Metaxa
¹/₂ measure/2 tsp ouzo
dash lemon juice
dash Angostura bitters
2 measures/3 tbsp dry sparkling wine
2 measures/3 tbsp sparkling ginger ale
slice of lemon, to garnish

1 Stir the first four ingredients in a jug (pitcher) with ice.

2 Strain into a tall glass and top up with the sparkling wine and ginger ale. Garnish with a slice of lemon.

Nutritional information per portion: Energy 107kcal/442kJ; Protein 0.1g; Carbohydrate 4g, of which sugars 4g; Fat 0g, of which saturates 0g; Cholesterol 0mg; Calcium 4mg; Fibre 0g; Sodium 2mg; Alcohol 13g.

Pisco Sour

The origin of pisco, the colourless brandy of South America, is energetically disputed between Peru and Chile. This is the classic way of taking it locally.

MAKES 1 GLASS

half a lime
5ml/1 tsp caster (superfine) sugar
2 measures/3 tbsp pisco
dash of Angostura bitters (optional)
slice of lime, to garnish

1 Half-fill a small tumbler with crushed ice. Squeeze the lime juice directly into the glass and drop in the wrung-out shell.

2 Add the sugar and stir well to dissolve it. Now add the pisco and give the drink a final stir. A dash of Angostura bitters can be added too, if desired.

3 Garnish with a slice of lime, threaded on to a cocktail stick (toothpick).

Nutritional information per portion: Energy 117kcal/485kJ; Protein 0.1g; Carbohydrate 4.4g, of which sugars 4.4g; Fat 0g, of which saturates 0g; Cholesterol 0mg; Calcium 3mg; Fibre 0g; Sodium 0mg; Alcohol 14.3g.

Torpedo

I have come across various different mixtures going under this title. This seems to me to be the one most worthy of the name. It's very dry, spirity and strong, and its name reflects something of the force with which it will go through you.

MAKES 1 GLASS

1¹/₂ measures/6 tsp cognac
³/₄ measure/3 tsp calvados
dash of gin
twist of lemon, to garnish

1 Shake all the liquid ingredients well with ice in a cocktail shaker.

2 Strain into a pre-chilled cocktail glass. Garnish with a twist of lemon.

Nutritional information per portion: Energy 100kcal/414kJ; Protein 0g; Carbohydrate 0g, of which sugars 0g; Fat 0g, of which saturates 0g; Cholesterol 0mg; Calcium 0mg; Fibre 0g; Sodium 0mg; Alcohol 14.3g.

Captain Kidd

Brandy and dark rum make a heady, but very successful mix in a powerful cocktail, and this one is further enhanced by the addition of strong chocolate flavour. There are no non-alcoholic ingredients, you'll notice, so watch out.

MAKES 1 GLASS

1¹/₂ measures/6 tsp cognac
1 measure/1¹/₂ tbsp dark rum
1 measure/1¹/₂ tbsp brown crème
  de cacao
physalis or half-slice of orange, to garnish

1 Shake the liquid ingredients well with ice in a cocktail shaker.

2 Strain into a chilled champagne saucer. Garnish with a physalis or a half-slice of orange.

Nutritional information per portion: Energy 185kcal/771kJ; Protein 0g; Carbohydrate 7.4g, of which sugars 7.4g; Fat 0g, of which saturates 0g; Cholesterol 0mg; Calcium 1mg; Fibre 0g; Sodium 3mg; Alcohol 22.6g.

Brandy Alexander

One of the greatest cocktails of them all, Alexander can be served at the end of a grand dinner with coffee as a creamy digestif, or as a stomach-lining first drink of the evening at a cocktail party.

MAKES 1 GLASS

1 measure/1¹/₂ tbsp cognac
1 measure/1¹/₂ tbsp brown crème de cacao
1 measure/1¹/₂ tbsp double (heavy) cream
ground nutmeg or grated dark (bittersweet) chocolate, to garnish

1 Shake the cognac, brown crème de cacau and double cream thoroughly with ice in a cocktail shaker.

2 Strain the drink into a cocktail glass. Sprinkle ground nutmeg on top. Alternatively, sprinkle with grated dark chocolate.

Nutritional information per portion: Energy 235kcal/970kJ; Protein 0.4g; Carbohydrate 5.5g, of which sugars 5.5g; Fat 15.6g, of which saturates 7.5g; Cholesterol 31mg; Calcium 15mg; Fibre 0g; Sodium 25mg; Alcohol 10.1g.

Frozen Strawberry Daiquiri

This is a spinoff version of the rum original. When the fresh fruit isn't in season, you can use drained, canned strawberries instead, but wash off the sugar syrup.

MAKES 1 GLASS

4 strawberries
1/2 measure/2 tsp lime juice
1 measure/11/2 tbsp cognac
1 measure/11/2 tbsp light rum
dash of grenadine
strawberry, to garnish

1 Put the strawberries, lime juice and cognac in a liquidizer. Process to a purée.

2 Add the light rum, grenadine and half a glass of finely crushed ice and process once more to a smooth slush.

3 Pour the resulting mixture into a well-chilled cocktail glass. Garnish with a strawberry.

Nutritional information per portion: Energy 114kcal/471kJ; Protein 0.4g; Carbohydrate 3g, of which sugars 3g; Fat 0g, of which saturates 0g; Cholesterol 0mg; Calcium 8mg; Fibre 0.5g; Sodium 3mg; Alcohol 14.3g.

Other Spirits and Liqueurs

In this section, we deal with the less well-known spirits. These will include the bitter aperitifs, such as Campari, as well as the concentrated bitters, such as Angostura; the apple brandies, such as France's calvados and America's applejack; and the traditional European fruit distillates, such as Kirsch (made from cherries) and slivovitz (plums). Despite their minority status, they play an integral part in the cocktail repertoire.

Pink Gin

The famous tipple of British naval officers, this is simply a neat, bittered gin. Classically, it should be made with Plymouth gin, for its milder aromatic quality and its naval associations.

MAKES 1 GLASS

6 drops Angostura bitter
2 measures/3 tbsp gin

1 Sprinkle the Angostura bitter into a goblet-shaped glass, roll it around to coat the inner surfaces, then dash it out.

2 Add ice-cold gin, which will then take on the faintest pink tint.

Nutritional information per portion: Energy 50kcal/207kJ; Protein 0g; Carbohydrate 0g, of which sugars 0g; Fat 0g, of which saturates 0g; Cholesterol 0mg; Calcium 0mg; Fibre 0g; Sodium 0mg; Alcohol 7.2g.

Rose

Although it looks delicately pink and sweet, the cocktail that this 1920s recipe actually produces is very dry, and would make a good aperitif.

MAKES 1 GLASS

1 measure/1¹/₂ tbsp Kirsch
1¹/₂ measures/6 tsp dry vermouth
dash of grenadine

1 Shake all the ingredients well with ice in a cocktail shaker.

2 Strain into a cocktail glass.

BARTENDING KNOW-HOW
Kirsch and cherry brandy are not interchangeable, since the former is drier than the latter, and colourless. Cherry brandy is also lower in alcohol.

Nutritional information per portion: Energy 103kcal/431kJ;
Protein 0g; Carbohydrate 6.4g, of which sugars 6.4g;
Fat 0g, of which saturates 0g; Cholesterol 0mg;
Calcium 2mg; Fibre 0g; Sodium 5mg; Alcohol 11.3g.

Depth Charge

This is one of several 1920s cocktails that owe their names to the World War, which was then still fresh in everyone's memory.

MAKES 1 GLASS

1 measure/1½ tbsp calvados
1 measure/1½ tbsp cognac
½ measure/2 tsp lemon juice
¼ measure/1 tsp grenadine
slice of red apple, to garnish

1 Shake all the liquid ingredients well with ice in a cocktail shaker.

2 Strain into a cocktail glass. Garnish with a slice of apple.

Nutritional information per portion: Energy 116kcal/483kJ; Protein 0g; Carbohydrate 1.4g, of which sugars 1.4g; Fat 0g, of which saturates 0g; Cholesterol 0mg; Calcium 1mg; Fibre 0g; Sodium 0mg; Alcohol 15.9g.

Apple Blossom

The slightly sweeter finish of applejack is better suited than calvados in this American cocktail. Use ordinary sugar syrup if you can't get hold of maple, although it won't be quite the same.

MAKES 1 GLASS

1¹/₂ measures/6 tsp applejack
1 measure/1¹/₂ tbsp apple juice
¹/₂ measure/2 tsp lemon juice
¹/₄ measure/1 tsp maple syrup
slice of red apple, to garnish

1 Shake all the liquid ingredients well with ice in a cocktail shaker.

2 Strain into a cocktail glass or champagne saucer. Garnish with the apple slice.

Nutritional information per portion: Energy 84kcal/350kJ; Protein 0g; Carbohydrate 5.4g, of which sugars 5.4g; Fat 0g, of which saturates 0g; Cholesterol 0mg; Calcium 2mg; Fibre 0g; Sodium 14mg; Alcohol 10.9g.

Americano

A recipe going back to the early years of the 20th century, Americano was the one of the first to make a feature of the bitter red Italian aperitivo, Campari.

MAKES 1 GLASS

2 measures/3 tbsp sweet red vermouth
1 measure/1¹/₂ tbsp Campari
1 measure/1¹/₂ tbsp soda water
twist of orange rind, to garnish

1 Add the first two ingredients to a rocks glass or Old-fashioned glass with two or three cubes of ice in it.

2 Stir, and add the soda.

3 Squeeze a twist of orange rind over the drink and then drop it in.

Nutritional information per portion: Energy 127kcal/531kJ; Protein 0g; Carbohydrate 14.5g, of which sugars 14.5g; Fat 0g, of which saturates 0g; Cholesterol 0mg; Calcium 4mg; Fibre 0g; Sodium 15mg; Alcohol 10g.

Negroni

The Negroni is an Americano with gin, making an altogether drier drink. It is named after Count Negroni who invented this formula in Florence just after the First World War.

MAKES 1 GLASS

2 measures/3 tbsp gin
1 measure/1¹/₂ tbsp sweet red vermouth
³/₄ measure/3 tsp Campari
1 measure/1¹/₂ tbsp soda water
twist of orange rind and a physalis,
to garnish

1 Mix the first three ingredients in a tumbler with ice.

2 Add the soda.

3 Squeeze a twist of orange rind over the drink and then drop it in. Garnish with a whole physalis.

Nutritional information per portion: Energy 173kcal/720kJ;
Protein 0g; Carbohydrate 8.5g, of which sugars 8.5g;
Fat 0g, of which saturates 0g; Cholesterol 0mg;
Calcium 2mg; Fibre 0g; Sodium 8mg; Alcohol 20.1g.

French Toddy

This is a variation of a very old French recipe, said to have been a favourite of the novelist Gustave Flaubert, to which coffee and sugar have been added. This recipe serves two.

MAKES 2 GLASSES

120ml/4fl oz calvados
50ml/2fl oz apricot brandy
20–30ml/4–6 tsp sugar, to taste
300ml/¹/₂ pint very strong coffee (filter/
**   cafetière brewed at about 45g/8 tbsp**
**   coffee per 500ml/17fl oz water)**
25ml/1¹/₂ tbsp double (heavy) cream

1 Very gently warm the calvados and apricot brandy together in a small pan over a low heat, and transfer to large balloon glasses.

2 Dissolve the sugar in the coffee and add to the liquor. Stir vigorously.

3 While the contents are still rotating from the stirring, pour the cream over the surface in a circular motion. Do not stir further, just sip and savour.

Nutritional information per portion: Energy 270kcal/1122kJ; Protein 0.6g; Carbohydrate 15.3g, of which sugars 14.8g; Fat 6.7g, of which saturates 4.2g; Cholesterol 17mg; Calcium 17mg; Fibre 0g; Sodium 4mg; Alcohol 2.2g.

Vruiça Rakia

*This is how slivovitz, the Balkan plum spirit, is often drunk in its regions of origin. It is a
cold-weather preparation intended to insulate the outdoor worker. This recipe serves two.*

MAKES 2 GLASSES

4 measures/6 tbsp slivovitz
10ml/2 tsp soft brown sugar
4 measures/6 tbsp water
blueberries, to garnish

1 Put the slivovitz, sugar and water in a small pan and bring nearly to the
boil, stirring to dissolve the sugar.

2 Pour into mugs or heatproof glasses, and garnish with blueberries skewered
on to a swizzle-stick. Drink while hot.

Nutritional information per portion: Energy 120kcal/498kJ; Protein 0.1g; Carbohydrate 5.2g, of which sugars 5.2g;
Fat 0g, of which saturates 0g; Cholesterol 0mg; Calcium 3mg; Fibre 0g; Sodium 1mg; Alcohol 14.3g.

Whip

This lethally violent 1920s cocktail contains a lot of strong alcohol and no mixers. Caution is advised – one should be more than enough.

MAKES 1 GLASS

1 measure/1¹/₂ tbsp cognac
¹/₂ measure/2 tsp dry vermouth
¹/₂ measure/2 tsp sweet red vermouth
¹/₄ measure/1 tsp orange curaçao
dash of absinthe

1 Shake all the ingredients well with plenty of ice in a cocktail shaker.

2 Strain into a cocktail glass.

Nutritional information per portion: Energy 89kcal/370kJ; Protein 0g; Carbohydrate 3.5g, of which sugars 3.5g; Fat 0g, of which saturates 0g; Cholesterol 0mg; Calcium 2mg; Fibre 0g; Sodium 5mg; Alcohol 10.9g.

Silver Jubilee

This was created for Queen Elizabeth's Silver Jubilee in 1977. There is a tendency now to up the gin quotient to as much as double this quantity, but I find that these proportions work perfectly well.

MAKES 1 GLASS

1 measure/1¹/₂ tbsp gin
1 measure/1¹/₂ tbsp crème de banane
1 measure/1¹/₂ tbsp double
    (heavy) cream
dark (bittersweet) chocolate,
    to garnish (optional)

1 Shake all the liquid ingredients thoroughly with ice in a cocktail shaker to amalgamate the cream.

2 Strain into a chilled cocktail glass. Grate a little dark chocolate over the surface, if desired.

BARTENDING KNOW-HOW
Cream cocktails should generally be made with double cream, as the single (light) version tends to be too runny.

Nutritional information per portion: Energy 246kcal/
1019kJ; Protein 0.4g; Carbohydrate 6.4g,
of which sugars 6.4g; Fat 17.3g, of which saturates 7.5g;
Cholesterol 33mg; Calcium 17mg; Fibre 0g; Sodium 32mg;
Alcohol 14g.

B52

This cocktail depends on the difference in specific weight or densities of each of the liqueurs to remain separated. Serve in a shot glass or liqueur glass.

MAKES 1 GLASS

1 measure/1¹/₂ tbsp Kahlúa
1 measure/1¹/₂ tbsp Bailey's Irish Cream
1 measure/1¹/₂ tbsp Grand Marnier

1 Pour the Kahlúa over the back of a cold teaspoon into a shot glass or liqueur glass.

2 Using a clean spoon, repeat with the Bailey's Irish Cream, and then, using another clean spoon, the Grand Marnier.

3 If you can't get the hang of the layering, just shake it all up with ice and strain it into a cocktail glass.

Nutritional information per portion: Energy 217kcal/904kJ; Protein 0g; Carbohydrate 15.8g, of which sugars 15.8g; Fat 7g, of which saturates 0g; Cholesterol 0mg; Calcium 8mg; Fibre 0g; Sodium 41mg; Alcohol 13.3g.

Hooded Claw

Syrupy-sweet prune juice with amaretto and Cointreau makes a delicious digestif when poured over a snow of finely crushed ice. This recipe serves four people.

MAKES 4 GLASSES

5 measures/120ml/4fl oz prune juice
2 measures/3 tbsp amaretto
1 measure/1¹/₂ tbsp Cointreau

1 Shake all the ingredients well with ice in a cocktail shaker.

2 Strain into four small liqueur glasses loosely filled with crushed ice.

Nutritional information per portion: Energy 74kcal/313kJ; Protein 0.2g; Carbohydrate 12g, of which sugars 12g; Fat 0.1g, of which saturates 0g; Cholesterol 0mg; Calcium 8mg; Fibre 0.9g; Sodium 7mg; Alcohol 4g.

Stratosphere

A few drops of crème de violette and a clove are added to a glass of champagne in this ladylike aperitif. An American violet liqueur, Crème Yvette, was at one time the only correct product to use, but Parfait Amour might also do.

MAKES 1 GLASS

1 glass champagne
few drops of crème de violette
1 clove

1 Add a few drops of crème de violette to a glass of champagne, drop at a time, until a mauve colour is obtained.

2 Add the whole clove to the drink, then serve immediately.

Nutritional information per portion: Energy 99kcal/411kJ; Protein 0.4g; Carbohydrate 7.2g, of which sugars 7.2g; Fat 0g, of which saturates 0g; Cholesterol 0mg; Calcium 11mg; Fibre 0g; Sodium 7mg; Alcohol 10g.

Oasis

Blue cocktails suddenly became all the rage during the cocktail boom of the 1980s. This is a particularly satisfying mixture that's not too sweet. Its stunning blue colour comes from blue curaçao. It is a perfect refreshing drink for a summer evening.

MAKES 1 GLASS

2 measures/3 tbsp gin
1/2 measure/2 tsp blue curaçao
4 measures/6 tbsp tonic water
slice of lemon and a sprig of mint,
    to garnish

1 Pour the gin into a highball glass half-filled with cracked ice.

2 Add the curaçao, top up with the tonic and stir gently.

3 Garnish with a slice of lemon and a sprig of mint.

Nutritional information per portion: Energy 137kcal/572kJ;
Protein 0g; Carbohydrate 10.3g, of which sugars 3.3g;
Fat 0g, of which saturates 0g; Cholesterol 0mg;
Calcium 1mg; Fibre 0g; Sodium 4mg; Alcohol 12.9g.

Snowball

This is the kind of cocktail generally considered safe to give to minors, as it resembles nothing so much as a rich milkshake. If you require more of a kick, add $^1/_2$ measure/2 tsp sweet brown cream sherry too.

MAKES 1 GLASS

2 measures/3 tbsp advocaat
5 measures/120ml/4fl oz ice-cold
**   sparkling lemonade**

1 Pour the advocaat into a highball glass half-filled with cracked ice.

2 Add the lemonade and stir gently.

BARTENDING KNOW-HOW
Snowball needs plenty of lemonade to avoid its texture being too cloying.

Nutritional information per portion: Energy 173kcal/720kJ; Protein 0g; Carbohydrate 17.2g, of which sugars 17.2g; Fat 7g, of which saturates 0g; Cholesterol 0mg; Calcium 14mg; Fibre 0g; Sodium 48mg; Alcohol 6.1g.

Airstrike

*This is a burning drink,
similar to the Italian tradition
of the flaming Sambuca.
It should be allowed to cool
slightly before drinking.
The star anise releases a
wonderful taste and aroma.*

MAKES 1 GLASS

2 measures/3 tbsp Galliano
1 measure/1½ tbsp cognac
1 star anise

1 Heat the Galliano and brandy in a
small pan until just warm.

2 Pour into a heat-resistant glass
and add the star anise.

3 Using a long match, pass the
flame over the surface of the drink
to ignite it, being careful not to
burn yourself.

4 Let it burn for a couple of
minutes, until the star anise has
begun to sizzle a little and released
its aroma into the drink.

5 Leave the cocktail to cool slightly
before drinking.

Nutritional information per portion: Energy 117kcal/482kJ;
Protein 0g; Carbohydrate 0g, of which sugars 0g; Fat 0g,
of which saturates 0g; Cholesterol 0mg; Calcium 0mg;
Fibre 0g; Sodium 0mg; Alcohol 16.6g.

Long Island Iced Tea

This is a long, powerful drink with a rumbustiously intoxicating effect, its potency well disguised by the cola. For a simpler version, use equal quantities of rum, Cointreau, tequila and lemon juice, and top up with cola. The recipe does not contain tea. It's a facetious way of referring to the fact that it looks innocuously like a glass of non-alcoholic iced tea.

MAKES 1 GLASS

¹/₂ **measure/2 tsp white rum**
¹/₂ **measure/2 tsp vodka**
¹/₂ **measure/2 tsp gin**
¹/₂ **measure/2 tsp silver tequila**
¹/₂ **measure/2 tsp Cointreau**
juice of half a lemon
¹/₂ **measure/2 tsp sugar syrup**
twist of lemon
4 measures/6 tbsp cola
sprig of fresh mint, to garnish

1 Stir the white rum, vodka, gin, sliver tequila, Cointreau, lemon juice and sugar syrup well with ice for about 30 seconds in a jug (pitcher) to chill.

2 Strain into a highball glass filled with ice cubes and a twist of lemon.

3 Add the chilled cola and finish with a sprig of fresh mint.

Nutritional information per portion: Energy 183kcal/762kJ; Protein 0g; Carbohydrate 15.5g, of which sugars 15.5g; Fat 0g, of which saturates 0g; Cholesterol 0mg; Calcium 6mg; Fibre 0g; Sodium 6mg; Alcohol 17.7g.

Singapore Sling

One of the all-time great cocktails, Singapore Sling was created in 1915 at the world-famous Raffles Hotel in Singapore. Some recipes omit the soda to give a slightly stronger drink. Some add a dash of grenadine just to deepen the pink colour, but it should nonetheless be no more than a fairly delicate blush.

MAKES 1 GLASS

2 measures/3 tbsp gin
2/3 measure/1 tbsp cherry brandy
2/3 measure/1 tbsp Cointreau
juice of 1 lemon
5ml/1 tsp caster (superfine) sugar
3 measures/4 1/2 tbsp soda water
twist of lemon peel and a black cherry,
   to garnish

1 Shake the gin, cherry brandy, Cointreau, lemon juice and caster sugar well with ice in a cocktail shaker.

2 Strain into a highball glass and add the soda.

3 Decorate the drink with the twist of lemon peel and a cherry pierced with two cocktail sticks (toothpicks).

Nutritional information per portion: Energy 203kcal/846kJ; Protein 0.1g; Carbohydrate 13.1g, of which sugars 13.1g; Fat 0g, of which saturates 0g; Cholesterol 0mg; Calcium 4mg; Fibre 0g; Sodium 1mg; Alcohol 21.9g.

Zam

This is a very resourceful cocktail that uses no fewer than three liqueurs, without the need for a plain spirit base. This enhances the herbal flavours well, and the overall effect is nicely balanced between sweet and dry.

MAKES 1 GLASS

1 measure/1¹/₂ tbsp Glayva
¹/₂ measure/2 tsp Bénédictine
¹/₂ measure/2 tsp Sambuca
1¹/₂ measures/6 tsp orange juice
¹/₄ measure/1 tsp sugar syrup
¹/₄ measure/1 tsp lemon juice
strawberry, to garnish

1 Shake all the liquid ingredients well with ice in a cocktail shaker

2 Strain into a chilled champagne saucer or wine goblet loaded with crushed ice.

3 Garnish with a strawberry.

Nutritional information per portion: Energy 114kcal/477kJ; Protein 0.2g; Carbohydrate 6.6g, of which sugars 6.6g; Fat 0g, of which saturates 0g; Cholesterol 0mg; Calcium 3mg; Fibre 0g; Sodium 4mg; Alcohol 12.7g.

Kir

This world-famous gastronomic aperitif was created in Burgundy and was originally named after a mayor of Dijon. The classic wine to use is a Bourgogne Aligoté of the most recent vintage, but any fairly neutral-tasting white wine will do, so long as it is sharp with acidity.

MAKES 1 GLASS

glass of light, dry, acidic white wine
¹/₄–¹/₂ measure/1–2 tsp crème de cassis

1 Stir the crème de cassis into the glass of wine.

2 Serve in a champagne glass.

BARTENDING KNOW-HOW
Add the cassis to a glass of non-vintage brut champagne and the drink becomes a Kir Royale.

Nutritional information per portion: Energy 129kcal/536kJ; Protein 0.2g, Carbohydrate 2.7g, of which sugars 2.7g, Fat 0g, of which saturates 0g; Cholesterol 0mg; Calcium 16mg; Fibre 0g; Sodium 8mg; Alcohol 16.9g.

Grand Slam

*This recipe uses punsch,
which mixes very suavely with
both shades of vermouth.
Here is an aperitif cocktail,
if ever there was one.*

MAKES 1 GLASS

2 measures/3 tbsp punsch
1 measure/1½ tbsp dry vermouth
1 measure/1½ tbsp sweet red vermouth

1 Stir all the ingredients well with
ice in a jug (pitcher).

2 Strain the cocktail over crushed
ice in a wine glass.

Nutritional information per portion: Energy 176kcal/738kJ;
Protein 0g; Carbohydrate 19g, of which sugars 19g;
Fat 0g, of which saturates 0g; Cholesterol 0mg;
Calcium 5mg; Fibre 0g; Sodium 14mg; Alcohol 15g.

Mad Monk

This is a cocktail I invented myself on first tasting the excellent hazelnut and herb liqueur, Frangelico, in its monk-shaped bottle.

MAKES 1 GLASS

1 measure/1¹/₂ tbsp gin
1 measure/1¹/₂ tbsp Frangelico
juice of half a lemon

1 Shake all the ingredients well with ice in a cocktail shaker.

2 Strain into a wine glass.

Nutritional information per portion: Energy 110kcal/459kJ; Protein 0g; Carbohydrate 7.6g, of which sugars 7.6g; Fat 0g, of which saturates 0g; Cholesterol 0mg; Calcium 2mg; Fibre 0g; Sodium 3mg; Alcohol 11.6g.

Sundowner

This recipe uses the bitter, orange-flavoured South African liqueur, Van der Hum. Instead of using cognac, though, you could substitute a good South African brandy if you come across it. Many of them are surprisingly fine in quality.

MAKES 1 GLASS

1¹/₂ measures/6 tsp cognac
1 measure/1¹/₂ tbsp Van der Hum
¹/₂ measure/2 tsp orange juice
¹/₂ measure/2 tsp lemon juice
physalis, to garnish

1 Shake all the liquid ingredients well with ice in a cocktail shaker.

2 Strain into a cocktail glass.

3 Garnish with a physalis.

Nutritional information per portion: Energy 117kcal/486kJ; Protein 0.1g; Carbohydrate 7.1g, of which sugars 7.1g; Fat 0g, of which saturates 0g; Cholesterol 0mg; Calcium 2mg; Fibre 0g; Sodium 3mg; Alcohol 7.6g.

Cara Sposa

Liqueurs and cream without the addition of a spirit base add up to a sweet, rich cocktail, and if that's your tipple, this luxurious creation is a well-nigh unbeatable one. Serve it at the end of dinner after a correspondingly light dessert.

MAKES 1 GLASS

1 measure/1¹/₂ tbsp Tia Maria
1 measure/1¹/₂ tbsp Cointreau
¹/₂ measure/2 tsp double (heavy) cream
twist of orange, to garnish

1 Shake all the liquid ingredients well with ice in a cocktail shaker.

2 Strain into a champagne saucer.

3 Garnish with a twist of orange.

Nutritional information per portion: Energy 144kcal/603kJ; Protein 0.2g; Carbohydrate 12.7g, of which sugars 12.7g; Fat 5.4g, of which saturates 3g; Cholesterol 13mg; Calcium 7mg; Fibre 0g; Sodium 8mg; Alcohol 11.1g.

Rite of Spring

Green cocktails that don't somehow taste of mint are few and far between. The relatively rare green curaçao is worth buying if you come across it, and here is a recipe of my own, tailor-made for it.

MAKES 1 GLASS

2 measures/3 tbsp vodka
1 measure/1½ tbsp green curaçao
4 measures/6 tbsp sparkling lemonade
long twist of lemon rind, to garnish

1 Mix the vodka and curaçao with ice in a jug (pitcher) until well-chilled.

2 Pour without straining into a highball glass, and top up with the lemonade.

3 Dangle a long twist of lemon rind in the drink.

Nutritional information per portion: Energy 179kcal/745kJ; Protein 0g; Carbohydrate 12.6g, of which sugars 12.6g; Fat 0g, of which saturates 0g; Cholesterol 0mg; Calcium 6mg; Fibre 0g; Sodium 9mg; Alcohol 18.7g.

Yellow Parrot

This is a powerful and colourful cocktail from the 1920s. It is essential to serve this drink over plenty of crushed ice, which will mitigate a little of its strength and firepower.

MAKES 1 GLASS

1 measure/1¹/₂ tbsp absinthe
1 measure/1¹/₂ tbsp yellow Chartreuse
1 measure/1¹/₂ tbsp apricot brandy

1 Shake all the ingredients well with ice in a cocktail shaker.

2 Strain into a cocktail glass filled almost to the brim with crushed ice. Do not garnish.

Nutritional information per portion: Energy 207kcal/862kJ; Protein 0g; Carbohydrate 7.3g, of which sugars 7.3g; Fat 0g, of which saturates 0g; Cholesterol 0mg; Calcium 0mg; Fibre 0g; Sodium 0mg; Alcohol 25.7g.

Midori Sour

The standard Sour treatment works quite well with Midori, and certainly makes for a more exotic alternative to yet another Whisky Sour, but it's better shaken than stirred.

MAKES 1 GLASS

2 measures/3 tbsp Midori
1 measure/1¹/₂ tbsp lemon juice
¹/₄ measure/1 tsp sugar syrup
melon ball, to garnish

1 Shake the Midori, lemon juice and sugar syrup well with ice in a cocktail shaker.

2 Strain into a tumbler.

3 Garnish with a melon ball.

BARTENDING KNOW-HOW
You may find that this cocktail is sufficiently sweet without the sugar syrup. You can leave it out or adjust the quantity to your liking.

Nutritional information per portion: Energy 125kcal/525kJ; Protein 0.1g; Carbohydrate 16.6g, of which sugars 16.6g; Fat 0g, of which saturates 0g; Cholesterol 0mg; Calcium 4mg; Fibre 0g; Sodium 6mg; Alcohol 8.6g.

Southern Peach

The peach notes in America's classic whiskey liqueur are accentuated by its being mixed with peach brandy in this cream cocktail.

MAKES 1 GLASS

1 measure/1¹/₂ tbsp Southern Comfort
1 measure/1¹/₂ tbsp peach brandy
1 measure/1¹/₂ tbsp double
   (heavy) cream
dash of Angostura bitters
wedge of ripe peach, to garnish

1 Shake all the liquid ingredients well with plenty of ice in a cocktail shaker.

2 Strain into a tumbler.

3 Garnish with a wedge of ripe peach, slicing it almost into three pieces, but leaving it intact at one end.

Nutritional information per portion: Energy 195kcal/811kJ; Protein 0.3g; Carbohydrate 9.1g, of which sugars 9.1g; Fat 10.2g, of which saturates 5.7g; Cholesterol 25mg; Calcium 10mg; Fibre 0g; Sodium 9mg; Alcohol 9.4g.

Milano

The assertive flavour of Galliano comes through strongly in this short, sour cocktail, which leaves a long but delicious aftertaste.

MAKES 1 GLASS

1 measure/1¹/₂ tbsp gin
1 measure/1¹/₂ tbsp Galliano
juice of half a lemon
cherry and a slice each of lemon and lime,
    to garnish

1 Shake all the liquid ingredients well with ice in a cocktail shaker.

2 Strain into a cocktail glass.

3 Garnish the drink with a cherry and slices of lemon and lime on a cocktail stick (toothpick).

Nutritional information per portion: Energy 111kcal/462kJ; Protein 0.1g; Carbohydrate 7.8g, of which sugars 7.8g; Fat 0g, of which saturates 0g; Cholesterol 0mg; Calcium 3mg; Fibre 0g; Sodium 3mg; Alcohol 11.6g.

Peugeot

This very French cocktail is intended, unexpectedly, as a tribute to the car manufacturer. Owners of their cars may drink it with pride, though not before driving anywhere, as it's quite strong.

MAKES 1 GLASS

1¹/₂ **measures/6 tsp Cointreau**
³/₄ **measure/3 tsp calvados**
2 measures/3 tbsp orange juice
slice of orange, to garnish

1 Shake the liquid ingredients well with ice in a cocktail shaker.

2 Strain into a cocktail glass.

3 Garnish with the orange slice, threaded on to a small skewer.

Nutritional information per portion: Energy 144kcal/601kJ; Protein 0.2g; Carbohydrate 11.3g, of which sugars 11.3g; Fat 0g, of which saturates 0g; Cholesterol 0mg; Calcium 5mg; Fibre 0g; Sodium 6mg; Alcohol 14.3g.

Blue Lady

This sweet, creamy cocktail combines the flavours of orange and chocolate in a most peculiar hue.

MAKES 1 GLASS

1½ **measures/6 tsp blue curaçao**
½ **measure/2 tsp white crème de cacao**
½ **measure/2 tsp double (heavy) cream**

1 Shake the ingredients thoroughly with ice in a cocktail shaker.

2 Strain the drink into a cocktail glass. Do not garnish.

Nutritional information per portion: Energy 161kcal/669kJ; Protein 0.2g; Carbohydrate 12.3g, of which sugars 12.3g; Fat 6.9g, of which saturates 3.3g; Cholesterol 14mg; Calcium 8mg; Fibre 0g; Sodium 15mg; Alcohol 7.2g.

Il Paradiso

This creamy, sumptuous, chocolate-orange cocktail has a nice balance of sweet and bitter flavours.

MAKES 1 GLASS

1 measure/1¹/₂ tbsp Tuaca
1 measure/1¹/₂ tbsp orange curaçao
1 measure/1¹/₂ tbsp double
 (heavy) cream
grated orange rind, to garnish

1 Shake all the liquid ingredients with ice in a cocktail shaker.

2 Strain into a cocktail glass. Alternatively, whizz it up in the blender for an extra-frothy texture.

3 Garnish the drink with grated orange rind.

Nutritional information per portion: Energy 175kcal/726kJ;
Protein 0.3g; Carbohydrate 6.7g, of which sugars 6.7g;
Fat 10.2g, of which saturates 5.7g; Cholesterol 25mg;
Calcium 10mg; Fibre 0g; Sodium 9mg; Alcohol 11.3g.

Café à l'Orange

This is one of numerous drink possibilities in which the flavours of orange and coffee are combined. The recipe serves four.

MAKES 4 GLASSES

120ml/4fl oz whipping cream
30ml/2 tbsp icing (confectioners') sugar
5ml/1 tsp grated orange rind
600ml/1 pint hot black coffee
150ml/¹/₄ pint any orange-flavoured liqueur, such as Grand Marnier, Cointreau, triple sec, etc
4 orange wedges, to garnish

1 In a clean bowl, whip the cream until stiff.

2 Fold in the icing sugar and rind.

3 Chill for 30 minutes, or until the cream mixture is firm enough to hold a wedge of orange on top.

4 Divide the black coffee equally among tall glass mugs.

5 Stir about 30ml/2 tbsp liqueur into each.

6 Top with chilled whipped cream and balance an orange wedge on top. Serve immediately.

Nutritional information per portion: Energy 262kcal/ 1089kJ; Protein 0.6g; Carbohydrate 17.8g, of which sugars 17.8g; Fat 12.1g, of which saturates 7.6g; Cholesterol 32mg; Calcium 22mg; Fibre 0g; Sodium 10mg; Alcohol 11.9g.

Highland Milk Punch

This is just the sort of thing to keep the cold at bay on chilly nights in the frozen north of Scotland, or anywhere else for that matter.

MAKES 1 GLASS

2 measures/3 tbsp Scotch
1 measure/1¹/₂ tbsp Drambuie
1 egg, beaten
250ml/8fl oz full cream (whole) milk
powdered cinnamon, to garnish

1 Put the Scotch, Drambuie, beaten egg and milk into a small pan and heat gently, stirring constantly to incorporate the egg and prevent the milk from burning on the bottom of the pan.

2 Just before the mixture boils, pour it into a glass mug.

3 Sprinkle the surface of the drink with powdered cinnamon.

Nutritional information per portion: Energy 409kcal/ 1700kJ; Protein 14.5g; Carbohydrate 16.7g, of which sugars 16.7g; Fat 15.3g, of which saturates 7.8g; Cholesterol 225mg; Calcium 324mg; Fibre 0g; Sodium 179mg; Alcohol 21.4g.

After-dinner Coffee

This is a superb Mexican way to end a meal. Kahlúa, the coffee liqueur used in this drink, is also delicious served in a liqueur glass topped with a thin layer of cream. This recipe serves four.

MAKES 4 CUPS

50g/2oz dark-roast ground coffee
475ml/16fl oz boiling water
120ml/4fl oz tequila
120ml/4fl oz Kahlúa
5ml/1 tsp natural vanilla extract
30ml/2 tbsp soft dark brown sugar
150ml/¼ pint double (heavy) cream

1 Put the coffee in a heatproof jug (pitcher) or cafetière, pour on the boiling water and leave until the coffee grounds settle at the bottom.

2 Strain the coffee into a clean heatproof jug. Add the tequila, Kahlúa and vanilla extract, and stir well to mix.

3 Add the sugar and continue to stir until it has dissolved completely.

4 Pour the mixture into small coffee cups or tall heat-resistant glasses.

5 Hold a spoon just above the surface of each coffee. Pour the cream very slowly down the back of the spoon so that it forms a pool on top. Serve immediately.

Nutritional information per portion: Energy 380kcal/ 1573kJ; Protein 0.6g; Carbohydrate 15.3g, of which sugars 15.3g; Fat 24.8g, of which saturates 12.5g; Cholesterol 51mg; Calcium 28mg; Fibre 0g; Sodium 36mg; Alcohol 13.6g.

White Hot Chocolate

This tasty new spin on hot chocolate matches white chocolate with orange liqueur for a creamy and warming drink. This recipe serves four.

MAKES 4 MUGS

1.75 litres/3 pints milk
175g/6oz white chocolate, broken into
    small pieces
1/2 measure/2 tsp coffee powder
4 measures/6 tbsp Cointreau or other
    orange-flavoured liqueur
whipped cream and ground cinnamon,
    to garnish

1 Heat the milk in a large heavy pan until almost boiling, then remove from the heat.

2 Add the white chocolate, coffee powder and liqueur.

3 Stir until all the white chocolate has melted.

4 Pour into four mugs. Top each with a spoonful of whipped cream and a sprinkling of ground cinnamon. Serve immediately.

Nutritional information per portion: Energy 591kcal/
2462kJ; Protein 18g; Carbohydrate 50.7g, of which
sugars 50.7g; Fat 30.6g, of which saturates 19g;
Cholesterol 61mg; Calcium 635mg; Fibre 0g;
Sodium 238mg; Alcohol 7.2g.

Champagne, Wines, Beer and Cider

Table wines are used seldom in cocktails as their flavours are so varied that it is hard to guarantee the results. For the following recipes, for a dry white wine, go for a light, unoaked Chardonnay, and for red, a Côtes du Rhône. The most resourceful fortified wine is vermouth with its herbal flavours. Sherry, port, Madeira and Marsala are also used. Beer and cider have a limited number of uses – the simplest beer 'cocktail' is shandy.

Spritzer

The most famous white wine cocktail is this simple creation. Everyone who drinks spritzers has his or her own preferred proportions, but this recipe should be reliable.

MAKES 1 GLASS

3 measures/4¹/₂ tbsp dry white wine
4 measures/6 tbsp soda water
mixed berries, to garnish (optional)

1 Half-fill a highball glass with cracked ice and add the wine.

2 Top up with the soda.

3 Garnish with mixed berries if you like, but the drink doesn't really need them.

Nutritional information per portion: Energy 38kcal/158kJ; Protein 0.1g; Carbohydrate 0.3g, of which sugars 0.3g; Fat 0g, of which saturates 0g; Cholesterol 0mg; Calcium 5mg; Fibre 0g; Sodium 2mg; Alcohol 5.3g.

Sonoma Cup

The Sonoma Valley in California produces some of the world's very best Chardonnays. However, a simpler white wine will do just as well.

MAKES 1 GLASS

3 measures/4¹/₂ tbsp dry white wine
¹/₂ measure/2 tsp Cointreau
3 measures/4¹/₂ tbsp orange juice
4 measures/6 tbsp soda water
twist of orange rind, to garnish

1 Shake the dry white wine, Cointreau and orange juice well with ice in a cocktail shaker.

2 Strain into a highball glass.

3 Add the soda, stir gently and garnish with a twist of orange rind.

Nutritional information per portion: Energy 90kcal/377kJ; Protein 0.3g; Carbohydrate 7.8g, of which sugars 7.8g; Fat 0.1g, of which saturates 0g; Cholesterol 0mg; Calcium 11mg; Fibre 0.1g; Sodium 9mg; Alcohol 8.4g.

Fantaisie

This appealing cocktail is best made with an off-dry or medium-dry white wine, rather than the very driest. An aromatic, floral-scented Gewurztraminer from the Alsace region would suit this simple recipe down to the ground.

MAKES 1 GLASS

4 measures/6 tbsp off-dry white wine
³/₄ measure/3 tsp apricot brandy

1 Pour the white wine into a well-chilled goblet.

2 Add the apricot brandy and stir well. No garnish is necessary.

Nutritional information per portion: Energy 81kcal/336kJ; Protein 0.1g; Carbohydrate 0.4g, of which sugars 0.4g; Fat 0g, of which saturates 0g; Cholesterol 0mg; Calcium 7mg; Fibre 0g; Sodium 3mg; Alcohol 11.7g.

Bordeaux Cocktail

A good way of disguising harshness in a young red wine, this recipe is classically made with a young claret from Bordeaux. Wine-tasters claim to find the taste of blackcurrant in the Cabernet Sauvignon grape that most claret contains, but you can make sure of that by adding the cassis.

MAKES 1 GLASS

2 measures/3 tbsp red Bordeaux
1 measure/1¹/₂ tbsp cognac
³/₄ measure/3 tsp crème de cassis

1 Stir all the ingredients well with ice in a jug (pitcher).

2 Strain into a large wine glass. Do not garnish.

Nutritional information per portion: Energy 101kcal/421kJ; Protein 0.1g; Carbohydrate 5g, of which sugars 5g; Fat 0g, of which saturates 0g; Cholesterol 0mg; Calcium 3mg; Fibre 0g; Sodium 5mg; Alcohol 9.9g.

Sangria

Testament to the Spanish influence on Mexican cooking, this popular, thirst-quenching cocktail is traditionally served in large jugs to share, with ice and citrus fruit slices floating on top. It is a perfectly refreshing drink on a hot day. This recipe will serve six people.

MAKES 6 GLASSES

750ml/1¼ pints red wine
juice of 2 limes
4 measures/6 tbsp orange juice
4 measures/6 tbsp brandy
50g/2oz caster (superfine) sugar
1 lime, sliced, to garnish

1 Combine the wine, lime juice, orange juice and brandy in a large glass jug (pitcher).

2 Stir in the sugar until it has dissolved completely.

3 Serve in tall glasses with ice. Garnish each glass with a slice of lime.

Nutritional information per portion: Energy 144kcal/601kJ; Protein 0.2g; Carbohydrate 9.8g, of which sugars 9.8g; Fat 0g, of which saturates 0g; Cholesterol 0mg; Calcium 14mg; Fibre 0g; Sodium 10mg; Alcohol 15.1g.

Champagne Cocktail

The original champagne cocktail is an American recipe dating from the 19th century, although nobody appears to know precisely when it was first invented. I would use only a relatively inexpensive, non-vintage wine. As a rule, the very best stuff should never be mixed.

MAKES 1 GLASS

1 sugar cube
2 dashes Angostura bitters
¹/₄ measure/1 tsp cognac
champagne

1 Drop the sugar cube into a champagne flute, and add the Angostura, rolling the sugar lump to soak it.

2 Pour in the brandy, and then top the glass up with freshly opened champagne.

Nutritional information per portion: Energy 156kcal/650kJ; Protein 0.5g, Carbohydrate 13.1g, of which sugars 13.1g; Fat 0g, of which saturates 0g; Cholesterol 0mg; Calcium 18mg; Fibre 0g; Sodium 9mg; Alcohol 14.8g.

Operator

Another low-alcohol preparation, Operator is a rather more satisfying drink than the basic Spritzer, although along the same lines. It has a much more interesting taste than a Spritzer, which to my mind can only be a good thing.

MAKES 1 GLASS

2 measures/3 tbsp dry white wine
2 measures/3 tbsp sparkling ginger ale
¹/₄ measure/1 tsp lime juice
slice of lime, to garnish

1 Half-fill a rocks glass with cracked ice, then add all the liquid ingredients.

2 Stir the drink, then garnish with the slice of lime.

Nutritional information per portion: Energy 37kcal/153kJ; Protein 0.1g; Carbohydrate 2.1g, of which sugars 2.1g; Fat 0g, of which saturates 0g; Cholesterol 0mg; Calcium 4mg; Fibre 0g; Sodium 2mg; Alcohol 4.1g.

Marilyn Monroe

The drink named in honour of one of the great screen sirens of all time should really be made not just with champagne, but with the premium brand Dom Pérignon. It is fearfully expensive, though. Moet & Chandon Brut Impérial, made by the same house, might suffice instead.

MAKES 1 GLASS

4 measures/6 tbsp well-chilled champagne
1 measure/1¹/₂ tbsp applejack or calvados
¹/₄ measure/1 tsp grenadine
cocktail cherries, to garnish

1 Add all the liquid ingredients to a champagne saucer.

2 Stir extremely gently, then garnish with a couple of cocktail cherries on the rim of the glass.

Nutritional information per portion: Energy 130kcal/538kJ;
Protein 0.3g; Carbohydrate 6.2g, of which sugars 6.2g;
Fat 0g, of which saturates 0g; Cholesterol 0mg;
Calcium 8mg; Fibre 0g; Sodium 5mg; Alcohol 15g.

Southern Champagne

Southern Comfort is one of the foremost American liqueurs, and in the southern states of America, this is how they like a champagne cocktail to be. There is no need to use expensive champagne.

MAKES 1 GLASS

**1 measure/1¹/₂ tbsp Southern Comfort
dash of Angostura bitters
ice-cold champagne or sparkling wine
small twist of orange rind, to garnish**

1 Add the liqueur and bitters to a champagne flute.

2 Mix briefly and top up with champagne or sparkling wine.

3 Squeeze a small twist of orange rind over the drink, and then drop it into the glass.

Nutritional information per portion: Energy 200kcal/833kJ;
Protein 0.5g; Carbohydrate 14.4g, of which sugars 14.4g;
Fat 0g, of which saturates 0g; Cholesterol 0mg;
Calcium 16mg; Fibre 0g; Sodium 10mg; Alcohol 20.4g.

Sparkling Peach Melba

This refreshing fruit fizz is a great choice for summer celebrations. As with most soft fruit recipes, its success depends on using the ripest peaches and raspberries available. This recipe serves four.

MAKES 4 GLASSES

3 ripe peaches
90ml/6 tbsp orange juice
75g/3oz raspberries
10ml/2 tsp icing (confectioners') sugar
about 500ml/17fl oz raspberry sorbet
about 400ml/14fl oz medium sparkling
    wine, chilled

1 Put the peaches in a heatproof bowl and cover with boiling water. Leave for a minute, then drain and peel off the skins. Cut the fruit in half and remove the stones (pits). Chop the peach halves roughly and purée them with the orange juice in a blender until smooth. Transfer to a bowl.

2 Put the raspberries in the blender with the icing sugar and process until smooth. Press the raspberry purée through a sieve (strainer) into a separate bowl. Chill both purées for at least an hour.

3 Spoon the chilled peach purée into four tall glasses. Add scoops of sorbet to fill the glasses. Spoon the raspberry purée around the sorbet. Top up each glass with sparkling wine.

Nutritional information per portion: Energy 131kcal/551kJ; Protein 1.3g; Carbohydrate 14.7g, of which sugars 14.5g; Fat 0.2g, of which saturates 0g; Cholesterol 0mg; Calcium 17mg; Fibre 1.4g; Sodium 9mg; Alcohol 10.2g.

Bronx

An utterly satisfying mixture of gin and both vermouths, Bronx is, as the name suggests, a New York cocktail. It dates back to the early 20th century.

MAKES 1 GLASS

1¹/₂ measures/6 tsp gin
³/₄ measure/3 tsp dry vermouth
³/₄ measure/3 tsp sweet red vermouth
juice of a quarter of an orange
half-slice of orange, to garnish

1 Shake all the liquid ingredients well with ice in a cocktail shaker.

2 Strain into a cocktail glass.

3 To garnish, cut the half-slice of orange into half again, and thread on to a cocktail stick (toothpick).

Nutritional information per portion: Energy 111kcal/461kJ; Protein 0.1g; Carbohydrate 4.2g, of which sugars 4.2g; Fat 0g, of which saturates 0g; Cholesterol 0mg; Calcium 3mg; Fibre 0g; Sodium 7mg; Alcohol 13.6g.

Boston

This is an egg yolk recipe that contains a little sugar too, although the underlying mixture is nevertheless quite dry. Sprinkle grated nutmeg on top to enhance the warming flavours.

MAKES 1 GLASS

1¹/₂ **measures/6 tsp dry (sercial) Madeira**
1¹/₂ **measures/6 tsp bourbon**
2.5ml/¹/₂ **tsp caster (superfine) sugar**
1 **egg yolk**
grated nutmeg, to garnish

1 Shake the Madeira, bourbon, sugar and egg yolk with ice in a cocktail shaker.

2 Strain into a small wine glass.

3 Sprinkle with grated nutmeg and serve immediately.

Nutritional information per portion: Energy 178kcal/740kJ; Protein 3g, Carbohydrate 4.7g, of which sugars 4.7g, Fat 5.5g, of which saturates 1.6g; Cholesterol 202mg; Calcium 27mg; Fibre 0g; Sodium 13mg; Alcohol 14.1g.

Midsummer Night

The orangey, quinine flavour of Italian Punt e Mes goes well with gin and a modest amount of blackcurrant liqueur in this modern recipe.

MAKES 1 GLASS

1 measure/1¹/₂ tbsp gin
1 measure/1¹/₂ tbsp Punt e Mes
¹/₂ measure/2 tsp crème de cassis

1 Shake all the ingredients well with ice in a cocktail shaker.

2 Strain into a cocktail glass.

Nutritional information per portion: Energy 149kcal/623kJ;
Protein 0g; Carbohydrate 9.1g, of which sugars 9.1g;
Fat 0g, of which saturates 0g; Cholesterol 0mg;
Calcium 1mg; Fibre 0g; Sodium 3mg; Alcohol 16.4g.

Bamboo

An exceedingly dry aperitif cocktail, with a slight bittering element, this makes a change from the usual neat dry sherry. If you have it, you could use orange bitters instead of the Angostura version.

MAKES 1 GLASS

2 measures/3 tbsp pale dry (fino) sherry
2 measures/3 tbsp dry vermouth
2 dashes Angostura bitters

1 Stir all the ingredients well with ice in a jug (pitcher).

2 Strain into a chilled cocktail glass.

Nutritional information per portion: Energy 101kcal/420kJ;
Protein 0.1g; Carbohydrate 2g, of which sugars 2g;
Fat 0g, of which saturates 0g; Cholesterol 0mg;
Calcium 6mg; Fibre 0g; Sodium 9mg; Alcohol 13.3g.

Casanova

Marsala, from the island of Sicily, comes in various styles, but everyone seems agreed that the sweet version, dolce, is the best. That is what's used in this strong cream cocktail.

MAKES 1 GLASS

1 measure/1¹/₂ tbsp bourbon
¹/₂ measure/2 tsp Marsala dolce
¹/₂ measure/2 tsp Kahlúa
1 measure/1¹/₂ tbsp double
   (heavy) cream
ground nutmeg, to garnish

1 Shake the bourbon, Marsala, Kahlúa and cream well with plenty of ice in a cocktail shaker to amalgamate the cream.

2 Strain into a cocktail glass and sprinkle the top with ground nutmeg.

Nutritional information per portion: Energy 208kcal/858kJ; Protein 0.4g; Carbohydrate 3.4g, of which sugars 3.4g; Fat 13.6g, of which saturates 7.5g; Cholesterol 31mg; Calcium 14mg; Fibre 0g; Sodium 15mg; Alcohol 10g.

Sherry Flip

The recipe for a Flip would seem to go back to the 17th century. In the pre-cocktail-shaker era, they were mixed by being repeatedly poured, or 'flipped', between two glasses.

MAKES 1 GLASS

2 measures/3 tbsp brown cream sherry
2.5ml/¹⁄₂ tsp caster (superfine) sugar
1 egg, beaten
grated nutmeg, to garnish

1 Shake the sherry, sugar and egg well with ice in a cocktail shaker.

2 Strain into a small wine glass and sprinkle grated nutmeg on the surface. Alternatively, you can whizz it up in the blender.

Nutritional information per portion: Energy 123kcal/514kJ; Protein 6.3g; Carbohydrate 3.1g, of which sugars 3.1g; Fat 5.5g, of which saturates 1.6g; Cholesterol 190mg; Calcium 32mg; Fibre 0g; Sodium 74mg; Alcohol 5.4g.

Dubonnet Fizz

This American recipe makes for a sweetly aromatic cocktail. High rollers might fill it up with champagne, but soda will do quite nicely, thank you.

MAKES 1 GLASS

4 measures/6 tbsp red Dubonnet
$1/2$ measure/2 tsp cherry brandy
2 measures/3 tbsp orange juice
1 measure/$1^1/2$ tbsp lemon juice
soda water or champagne

1 Shake the red Dubonnet, cherry brandy, orange juice and lemon juice well with ice in a cocktail shaker.

2 Strain into a highball glass. Top up with soda water or champagne.

Nutritional information per portion: Energy 164kcal/687kJ; Protein 0.5g; Carbohydrate 13.4g, of which sugars 13.4g; Fat 0g, of which saturates 0g; Cholesterol 0mg; Calcium 11mg; Fibre 0g; Sodium 16mg; Alcohol 16g.

Inigo Jones

Here is the only cocktail in this book to use rosé wine. Choose one from a southern hemisphere country such as South Africa or Argentina – they tend to be fruitier than the European ones.

MAKES 1 GLASS

1 measure/1¹/₂ tbsp Marsala dolce
1 measure/1¹/₂ tbsp dry rosé wine
1 measure/1¹/₂ tbsp cognac
dash of orange juice
dash of lemon juice
slice of orange, to garnish

1 In a jug (pitcher), stir together all the liquid ingredients with plenty of ice.

2 Strain into a tumbler half-filled with crushed ice.

3 Garnish with the slice of orange.

Nutritional information per portion: Energy 98kcal/408kJ;
Protein 0.1g; Carbohydrate 2.6g, of which sugars 2.6g;
Fat 0g, of which saturates 0g; Cholesterol 0mg;
Calcium 5mg; Fibre 0g; Sodium 4mg; Alcohol 12.6g.

Parkeroo

This is a dry and rather startling mixture, which is worth trying at least once, just so you can say you have. I can't say it's one of my own favourites, but who's asking?

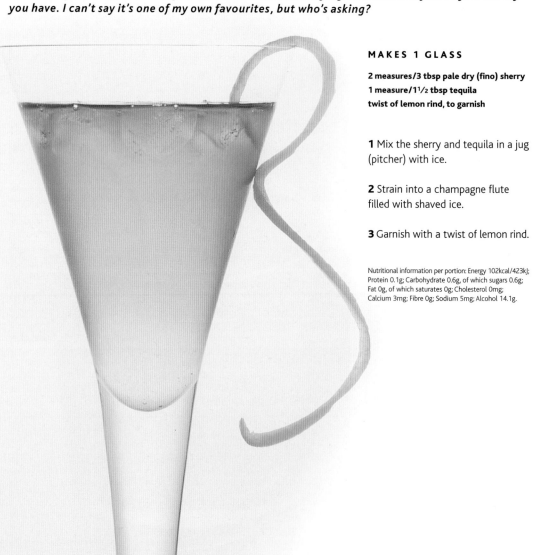

MAKES 1 GLASS

2 measures/3 tbsp pale dry (fino) sherry
1 measure/1½ tbsp tequila
twist of lemon rind, to garnish

1 Mix the sherry and tequila in a jug (pitcher) with ice.

2 Strain into a champagne flute filled with shaved ice.

3 Garnish with a twist of lemon rind.

Nutritional information per portion: Energy 102kcal/423kJ; Protein 0.1g; Carbohydrate 0.6g, of which sugars 0.6g; Fat 0g, of which saturates 0g; Cholesterol 0mg; Calcium 3mg; Fibre 0g; Sodium 5mg; Alcohol 14.1g.

Merry Widow

This is another 1920s recipe, this time at the bone-dry end of the spectrum, notwithstanding that splash of Bénédictine. It's a strong one too, all alcohol, which explains the merriness of the widow.

MAKES 1 GLASS

1 measure/1¹/₂ tbsp gin
1 measure/1¹/₂ tbsp dry vermouth
2 dashes of absinthe
2 dashes of Bénédictine
2 dashes of Angostura bitters
strip of lemon rind, to garnish

1 Stir all the liquid ingredients well with ice in a jug (pitcher).

2 Strain into a large wine glass.

3 Tie the strip of lemon rind into a decorative knot to garnish.

Nutritional information per portion: Energy 96kcal/397kJ;
Protein 0g; Carbohydrate 1.9g, of which sugars 1.9g;
Fat 0g, of which saturates 0g; Cholesterol 0mg;
Calcium 2mg; Fibre 0g; Sodium 3mg; Alcohol 12.6g.

Reform

This cocktail is so named as it was invented at the Reform Club in London in the 1920s.

MAKES 1 GLASS

2 measures/3 tbsp pale dry (fino) sherry
1 measure/1¹/₂ tbsp dry vermouth
dash of orange bitters (or curaçao)
cherry, to garnish

1 Stir the liquid ingredients well with ice in a jug (pitcher).

2 Strain into a cocktail glass and garnish with a cherry.

BARTENDING KNOW-HOW

Pale dry sherry should always be treated with kid gloves. It needs drinking within a few days of the bottle being broached, and should always be served well chilled.

Nutritional information per portion: Energy 77kcal/318kJ; Protein 0.1g; Carbohydrate 1.3g, of which sugars 1.3g; Fat 0g, of which saturates 0g; Cholesterol 0mg; Calcium 5mg; Fibre 0g; Sodium 7mg; Alcohol 10g.

Caffè Vermouth

Vermouth is not an obvious choice to partner coffee, but the result is original and sophisticated.

MAKES 2 GLASSES

4 measures/6 tbsp sweet red vermouth
60ml/4 tbsp very strong cold coffee
   (espresso strength or filter/cafetière
   brewed at 75g/3oz coffee per
   1 litre/1¾ pints water)
250ml/8fl oz milk
10ml/2 tsp caster (superfine) sugar
10-12 roasted coffee beans, to garnish

1 Shake the vermouth, coffee, milk and sugar well with ice in a cocktail shaker.

2 Strain the drink into cocktail glasses or tumblers. Garnish with roasted coffee beans.

Nutritional information per portion: Energy 145kcal/612kJ; Protein 4.3g; Carbohydrate 18.3g, of which sugars 18.3g; Fat 2.2g, of which saturates 1.4g; Cholesterol 7mg; Calcium 156mg; Fibre 0g; Sodium 67mg; Alcohol 5.9g.

Lamb's Wool

A kind of 17th-century punch, this cocktail was traditionally drunk on All Saints' Day, November 1. This recipe serves four. It's a real treat that will warm you up on a dark autumn day.

MAKES 4 GLASSES

1 litre/1³/₄ pints English bitter ale
4 baked apples
2.5ml/¹/₂ tsp ground nutmeg
2.5ml/¹/₂ tsp ground ginger
60g/2oz sugar

1 Heat the ale gently in a large pan without boiling it.

2 Peel the baked apples, remove the cores and mash the soft flesh with a potato masher.

3 Stir the apple into the beer with the spices and sugar.

4 Serve in warm glasses or mugs.

Nutritional information per portion: Energy 175kcal/741kJ; Protein 1.3g; Carbohydrate 30.8g, of which sugars 30.3g; Fat 0.3g, of which saturates 0g; Cholesterol 0mg; Calcium 34mg; Fibre 1.6g; Sodium 23mg; Alcohol 7.6g.

Black Velvet

This simple drink was invented at Brooks' Club in London in 1861, following the death of Prince Albert. It was considered an appropriate sign of mourning to dress the champagne up in black livery.

MAKES 1 GLASS

150ml/¼ pint/²/₃ cup Guinness
brut champagne

1 Half-fill a tall, narrow beer glass with Guinness.

2 Wait for the head to settle, and then, without tilting the glass, gently top it up with good brut champagne.

Nutritional information per portion: Energy 104kcal/433kJ;
Protein 0.7g; Carbohydrate 6.6g, of which sugars 6.6g;
Fat 0g, of which saturates 0g; Cholesterol 0mg;
Calcium 13mg; Fibre 0g; Sodium 11mg; Alcohol 10.8g.

Cider Cup

A long and refreshing aperitif – this drink (pictured right) should be prepared just before serving so that the ice doesn't melt.

MAKES 6 GLASSES

rind of 1 lemon
slices of orange
5 measures/120ml/4fl oz pale dry (fino) sherry
3 measures/4¹/₂ tbsp cognac
3 measures/4¹/₂ tbsp white curaçao
2 measures/3 tbsp amaretto
600ml/1 pint good-quality strong dry cider
twist of cucumber rind, to garnish

1 Partially fill a jug (pitcher) with cracked ice and stir in the lemon rind and the orange slices.

2 Add the sherry, brandy, curaçao and amaretto, and stir well to mix. Pour in the cider and stir gently.

3 Serve the cocktail in chilled tall glasses, including some of the citrus fruit in each one, and add a twist of cucumber rind.

Nutritional information per portion: Energy 137kcal/574kJ; Protein 0g; Carbohydrate 8.4g, of which sugars 8.4g; Fat 0g, of which saturates 0g; Cholesterol 0mg; Calcium 10mg; Fibre 0g; Sodium 11mg; Alcohol 15.1g.

Devon Gin

This is a short individual drink that will prove peculiarly potent on a cold winter's day. Be warned to tread cautiously.

MAKES 1 GLASS

3 measures/4¹/₂ tbsp strong sweet cider
³/₄ measure/3 tsp gin
¹/₄ measure/1 tsp Cointreau

1 Half-fill a rocks glass with cracked ice, and add the sweet cider and gin.

2 Stir gently, and then pour the Cointreau carefully on to the surface to form a float. Drink quickly.

BARTENDING KNOW-HOW
The best ciders are those that come in a bottle with a champagne-style cork. They may be cloudy, but the quality is incomparable.

Nutritional information per portion: Energy 77kcal/322kJ; Protein 0g; Carbohydrate 4.1g, of which sugars 4.1g; Fat 0g, of which saturates 0g; Cholesterol 0mg; Calcium 5mg; Fibre 0g; Sodium 5mg; Alcohol 9.5g.

Non-alcoholic Drinks

Not every cocktail session has to involve intoxication. The non-alcoholic section of many cocktail books often has an air of 'these are the also-rans' about it. That is not so here. There are enough recipes here to keep even the most determined mixologist going for a fair old time and, even more than their alcohol-based cousins, these drinks can be freely adapted as you see fit. Let your imagination off the leash.

Steel Works

This thirst-quenching drink can be served at any time of the day, but its sumptuous passion fruit flavours make it ideal for a summer afternoon.

MAKES 1 GLASS

2 measures/3 tbsp passion fruit juice
dash of Angostura bitters
3 measures/4¹/₂ tbsp soda water, chilled
3 measures/4¹/₂ tbsp lemonade, chilled
1 passion fruit

1 Pour the passion fruit juice into a tumbler and add the Angostura, with some ice cubes.

2 Finish the drink by adding the chilled soda water and lemonade, and stir briefly.

3 Cut the passion fruit in half; scoop out the seeds and flesh and add to the drink. Stir gently before serving.

VARIATION

For a Rock Shandy, pour equal parts of lemonade and soda over bitters or use your favourite variety of the naturally flavoured and unsweetened fruit drinks.

Nutritional information per portion: Energy 39kcal/165kJ; Protein 0.5g; Carbohydrate 9.5g, of which sugars 9.5g; Fat 0.1g, of which saturates 0g; Cholesterol 0mg; Calcium 9mg; Fibre 0.5g; Sodium 11mg; Alcohol 0g.

Blushing Piña Colada

This recipe doesn't contain the rum from the classic drink. Don't put whole ice cubes into the blender – make sure you crush them well first.

MAKES 2 GLASSES

1 banana, peeled and sliced
1 thick slice pineapple, peeled
3 measures/4^1/$_2$ tbsp pineapple juice
1 scoop strawberry ice cream or sorbet
1 measure/1^1/$_2$ tbsp unsweetened coconut milk
30ml/2 tbsp grenadine
cherry, to garnish

1 Roughly chop the banana. Cut two small wedges from the pineapple and set aside. Cut up the remainder of the pineapple and add it to the blender with the banana. Add the pineapple juice and process until smooth.

2 Add the ice cream or sorbet with the coconut milk and a little finely crushed ice, and process until smooth.

3 Pour into two large cocktail glasses. Pour the grenadine syrup slowly on top of the drink; it will filter down, creating a dappled effect. Garnish each glass with a wedge of pineapple and a cherry.

Nutritional information per portion: Energy 121kcal/515kJ; Protein 0.9g; Carbohydrate 30.4g, of which sugars 29g; Fat 0.4g, of which saturates 0.1g; Cholesterol 0mg; Calcium 21mg; Fibre 1.1g; Sodium 21mg; Alcohol 0g.

Horse's Fall

This is a long drink (pictured right) to serve on a summer's day. The addition of strongly flavoured tea is a matter of taste.

MAKES 1 GLASS

1 lemon
dash of Angostura bitters
2 measures/3 tbsp raspberry, Orange Pekoe or
    Assam tea, chilled (optional)
1 measure/1½ tbsp unsweetened apple juice
5 measures/120ml/4fl oz dry ginger ale
    or lemonade

1 Cut the rind from the lemon in one continuous strip and use it to line and decorate a long cocktail glass. Chill the glass until needed.

2 Add a dash of Angostura to the bottom of the chilled glass when you are ready to make the drink.

3 Measure the tea, if using, into the cocktail shaker and add the apple juice. Shake for about 20 seconds.

4 Strain into the prepared chilled glass. Finish with ginger ale or lemonade straight from the refrigerator, to taste.

Nutritional information per portion: Energy 27kcal/111kJ; Protein 0g; Carbohydrate 6.9g, of which sugars 6.9g; Fat 0g, of which saturates 0g; Cholesterol 0mg; Calcium 2mg; Fibre 0g; Sodium 0mg; Alcohol 0g.

Scarlet Lady

On the first sip, with its fruity and fresh tones, this drink could fool a fair few into thinking it was an alcoholic wine-based cocktail.

MAKES 1 GLASS

125g/4oz cubed melon, preferably Galia or Canteloupe
5 small red seedless grapes
3 measures/4½ tbsp unsweetened red grape juice

FOR THE GARNISH

3 small red seedless grapes
1 egg white, lightly beaten
15ml/1 tbsp sugar

1 Put the melon and grapes in a blender and process until they form a smooth purée.

2 Add the red grape juice and continue to process for another minute.

3 Strain the juice into a bar glass of ice and stir until chilled. Pour into a chilled cocktail glass.

4 To make the garnish, dip the red, seedless grapes in the lightly beaten egg white, and then into the sugar. Thread them on to a cocktail stick (toothpick).

Nutritional information per portion: Energy 67kcal/286kJ; Protein 0.9g; Carbohydrate 16.4g, of which sugars 16.4g; Fat 0.2g, of which saturates 0g; Cholesterol 0mg; Calcium 30mg; Fibre 0.6g; Sodium 44mg; Alcohol 0g.

Virgin Prairie Oyster

This cocktail (pictured right) really is a superior pick-me-up. The tomato base can be drunk without the raw egg yolk if it does not appeal to you. Use only fresh free-range eggs.

MAKES 1 GLASS

175ml/6fl oz tomato juice
1/2 measure/2 tsp Worcestershire sauce
1/4–1/2 measure/1–2 tsp balsamic vinegar
1 egg yolk
cayenne pepper, to taste

1 Measure the tomato juice into a large bar glass and stir over plenty of ice until well chilled.

2 Strain into a tall tumbler half-filled with ice cubes.

3 Add the Worcestershire sauce and balsamic vinegar to taste and mix with a swizzle-stick.

4 Float the egg yolk on top and lightly dust with cayenne pepper.

Nutritional information per portion: Energy 92kcal/388kJ; Protein 4.4g; Carbohydrate 6.8g, of which sugars 6.7g; Fat 5.5g, of which saturates 1.6g; Cholesterol 202mg; Calcium 60mg; Fibre 1.1g; Sodium 532mg; Alcohol 0g.

Fennel Fusion

This combination of raw vegetables and apples makes a surprisingly delicious juice. Cabbage has natural anti-bacterial properties, while apples and fennel help to cleanse the system.

MAKES 1 GLASS

half a small red cabbage
half a fennel bulb
2 apples
2/3 measure/1 tbsp lemon juice

1 Roughly slice the cabbage and fennel, and quarter the apples.

2 Using a juice extractor, juice the vegetables and fruit.

3 Add the lemon juice to the juice mixture and stir.

4 Pour into a glass and serve.

Nutritional information per portion: Energy 31kcal/130kJ; Protein 0.9g; Carbohydrate 6.7g, of which sugars 6.7g; Fat 0.2g, of which saturates 0g; Cholesterol 0mg; Calcium 26mg; Fibre 2.3g; Sodium 7mg; Alcohol 0g.

St Clements

Oranges and lemons create a simple but thirst-quenching drink, which confirms that freshly squeezed fruit has a superior flavour to any of the ready-squeezed versions you can buy.

MAKES 1 GLASS

2 oranges
1 lemon
15ml/1 tbsp sugar, or to taste
75ml/5 tbsp water
slice each of orange and lemon, to garnish

1 Wash the oranges and lemons and then pare off the rind with a knife. Remove and discard the pith.

2 Put the rind in a pan with the sugar and water. Place over a low heat and stir gently until the sugar has dissolved. Remove from the heat and press the rind against the sides of the pan to release their oils. Cover the pan and allow to cool.

3 Remove and discard the rind. Purée the oranges and lemon, then pour the cooled citrus syrup over the pulp. Set aside for 2–3 hours to allow the flavours to infuse.

4 Strain the fruit pulp, pressing the solids in the sieve (strainer) to extract the juice. Pour into a tall glass filled with finely crushed ice, and decorate with slices of orange and lemon.

Nutritional information per portion: Energy 148kcal/631kJ; Protein 2.7g; Carbohydrate 36.1g, of which sugars 36.1g; Fat 0.2g, of which saturates 0g; Cholesterol 0mg; Calcium 121mg; Fibre 4.1g; Sodium 13mg; Alcohol 0g.

Bandrek

This is a rich and creamy version of a spicy Indonesian drink. Serve it warm or chilled. If you like, add a very fresh egg to the syrup and mix in the blender, and you'll have something like an egg-nog.

MAKES 1 GLASS

3 whole cloves
3 juniper berries, bruised
1 cinnamon stick
6 green cardamom pods, bruised
1 sugar cube
4 whole black peppercorns
2 measures/3 tbsp unsweetened
    coconut milk
3 measures/4¹/₂ tbsp full-cream
    (whole) milk
cinnamon stick and maraschino cherry,
    to garnish

1 Put the cloves, juniper berries, cinnamon, cardamom pods, sugar and peppercorns in a pan. Heat gently.

2 Add 175ml/6fl oz water and bring to the boil over a medium-high heat. Boil for 10 minutes, or until reduced to 30–45ml/2–3 tbsp of spicy syrup.

3 Remove from the heat and cool. Pour the syrup into a blender with the coconut milk and full-cream milk. Process until smooth.

4 Strain over cracked ice in a stemmed glass. Garnish with the cinnamon sticks and cherry.

Nutritional information per portion: Energy 70kcal/295kJ;
Protein 2.4g; Carbohydrate 9.4g, of which sugars 9.4g;
Fat 2.8g, of which saturates 1.8g; Cholesterol 9mg;
Calcium 95mg; Fibre 0g; Sodium 79mg; Alcohol 0g.

Fruit and Ginger Ale

This is an old English mulled drink, served chilled over ice. Of course it can be made with ready-squeezed apple and orange juices, but roasting the fruit with cloves gives a much better flavour.

MAKES 4–6 GLASSES

1 cooking apple
1 orange, scrubbed
1 lemon, scrubbed
20 whole cloves
7.5cm/3in piece fresh ginger, peeled
30g/1oz light brown sugar
375ml/13fl oz bitter lemon
wedges of orange peel, studded with
**   cloves, to garnish**

1 Preheat the oven to 200°C/400°F/ Gas 6. Score the apple around the middle and stud the orange and lemon with the cloves. Bake the fruits in the oven for about 25 minutes, until soft. Quarter the orange and lemon, and mash the apple, discarding the peel and the core.

2 Finely grate the ginger. Place the fruit and ginger in a bowl with the sugar. Add 300ml/½ pint boiling water. Using a spoon, squeeze the fruit to release more flavour. Cover and let sit for an hour until cool.

3 Strain into a jug (pitcher) of cracked ice and press the juices from the fruit using a spoon. Add the bitter lemon. Garnish with the orange wedges.

Nutritional information per portion: Energy 33kcal/140kJ; Protein 0.1g; Carbohydrate 8.7g, of which sugars 8.7g; Fat 0g, of which saturates 0g; Cholesterol 0mg; Calcium 3mg; Fibre 0.2g; Sodium 1mg; Alcohol 0g.

Strawberry Soother

Relax after a busy day with this comforting drink of strawberries blended with either peach or nectarine, which is rich in vitamin C and healing phytochemicals.

MAKES 1 GLASS

225g/8oz strawberries
1 peach or nectarine

1 Hull the strawberries, then quarter the peach or nectarine and pull out the stone (pit).

2 Cut the fruit flesh into rough slices or chunks.

3 Juice the fruit, using a juicer, or process in a food processor or blender for a thicker juice, and serve immediately.

Nutritional information per portion: Energy 84kcal/354kJ; Protein 2.5g; Carbohydrate 18.8g, of which sugars 18.8g; Fat 0.3g, of which saturates 0g; Cholesterol 0mg; Calcium 41mg; Fibre 3.5g; Sodium 14mg; Alcohol 0g.

Lemonade on Ice

Home-made lemonade has a fresh, tangy flavour, unmatched by bought drinks. The basic lemonade will keep in the refrigerator for 2 weeks.

MAKES 6 GLASSES

6 lemons, washed and dried thoroughly
225g/8oz caster (superfine) sugar
1.75 litres/3 pints boiling water

FOR EACH ICED DRINK
4 scoops lemon sorbet
thin lemon and lime slices
3 ice cubes, crushed
sprig of mint and half-slices of lemon
    and lime, to garnish

1 Pare the lemons thinly, avoiding the pith. Put the rind in a heatproof bowl. Add the sugar. Squeeze the lemons and set the juice aside. Pour the boiling water over the rinds and sugar. Stir until the sugar dissolves. Leave to cool. Stir in the lemon juice. Strain the lemonade into a large jug (pitcher) and chill.

2 Place four scoops of sorbet in each tall glass. Tuck some lemon and lime slices down the sides. Add the ice. Top up each glass with 200ml/7fl oz of lemonade. Garnish with mint sprigs and half-slices of lemon and lime.

Nutritional information per portion: Energy 257kcal/1099kJ; Protein 0.9g; Carbohydrate 67.7g, of which sugars 67.7g; Fat 0g, of which saturates 0g; Cholesterol 0mg; Calcium 22mg; Fibre 0g; Sodium 17mg; Alcohol 0g.

Georgia 'n' Ginger

This non-alcoholic cocktail is named after the US state of Georgia, which is famous for its peaches. It is a fruity, spicy and warming concoction.

MAKES 6 GLASSES

1 can (450–500g/1–1¼lb) sliced
   peaches in syrup
750ml/1¼ pints strong coffee
120ml/4fl oz whipping cream
25ml/1½ tbsp brown sugar
1.5ml/¼ tsp ground cinnamon
generous pinch ground ginger
whipped cream and grated orange
   rind, to garnish

1 Drain the peaches, retaining the syrup. Process half of the coffee and the peaches for 1 minute, in a blender.

2 In a clean bowl, whip the cream.

3 Put 250ml/8fl oz cold water, the sugar, cinnamon, ginger and peach syrup in a pan and bring to the boil over a medium heat, then reduce the heat and simmer for 1 minute.

4 Add the blended peaches and the remaining coffee to the pan and stir. Serve, topped with whipped cream and decorated with orange rind.

Nutritional information per portion: Energy 134kcal/
558kJ; Protein 0.8g; Carbohydrate 15.4g, of which
sugars 15.4g; Fat 8.1g, of which saturates 5.1g;
Cholesterol 21mg; Calcium 16mg; Fibre 0.7g; Sodium 8mg;
Alcohol 0g.

Sunburst

Bursting with freshness and vitamins, this fruity and healthy drink is a good early morning pick-me-up. This recipe makes two glasses.

MAKES 2 GLASSES

1 green apple, cored and chopped
3 carrots, peeled and chopped
1 mango, peeled and pitted
7 measures/150ml/¹⁄₄ pint orange juice, chilled
6 strawberries, hulled
slice of orange, to garnish

1 Place the apple, carrots and mango in a blender or food processor and process to a pulp.

2 Add the orange juice and strawberries and process again.

3 Strain well through a sieve (strainer), pressing out all the juice with the back of a wooden spoon. Discard any pulp left in the sieve.

4 Pour into tumblers filled with ice cubes and serve immediately, garnished with a slice of orange on the side of the glass.

Nutritional information per portion: Energy 146kcal/619kJ; Protein 2.3g; Carbohydrate 34.7g, of which sugars 33.8g; Fat 0.8g, of which saturates 0.2g; Cholesterol 0mg; Calcium 63mg; Fibre 6.7g; Sodium 50mg; Alcohol 0g.

Humzinger

This tropical cleanser will help boost the digestive system and the kidneys, making your eyes sparkle, your hair shine and your skin glow.

MAKES 1 GLASS

half a pineapple, peeled
1 small mango, peeled and pitted
half a small papaya, seeded and peeled

1 Use a sharp knife to remove any 'eyes' left in the pineapple, and cut all the fruit into rough chunks.

2 Using a juice extractor, juice the fruit. Alternatively, use a food processor or blender and process for 2–3 minutes until very smooth.

3 Pour into a tumbler and serve the drink immediately.

Nutritional information per portion: Energy 358kcal/ 1531kJ; Protein 4.2g; Carbohydrate 87.9g, of which sugars 87.5g; Fat 1.4g, of which saturates 0.1g; Cholesterol 0mg; Calcium 159mg; Fibre 15.3g; Sodium 26mg; Alcohol 0g.

Licuado de Melon

Among the most refreshing drinks Mexicans make, this cocktail is made with fruit extracts mixed with honey and chilled water. This recipe is enough for four.

MAKES 4 GLASSES

1 watermelon
1 litre/1³/₄ pints chilled water
juice of 2 limes
honey

1 Cut the watermelon flesh into chunks, discarding the black seeds. Cover with chilled water and leave for 10 minutes.

2 Tip the mixture into a large sieve (strainer) set over a bowl. Using a wooden spoon, press the fruit to extract all the liquid.

3 Stir in the lime juice and sweeten the drink with honey. Pour it into a jug (pitcher), add ice cubes and stir. Serve in tumblers.

Nutritional information per portion: Energy 152kcal/653kJ; Protein 1.9g; Carbohydrate 36.2g, of which sugars 36.2g; Fat 1.1g, of which saturates 0.4g; Cholesterol 0mg; Calcium 27mg; Fibre 0.4g; Sodium 9mg; Alcohol 0g.

Citrus Agua Fresca

This refreshing fruit juice is sold from street stalls in towns all over Mexico. The zesty, tangy flavours of citrus fruits are balanced by the addition of sugar. The recipe serves four.

MAKES 4 GLASSES

12 limes
3 oranges
2 grapefruit
600ml/1 pint water
75g/6 tbsp caster (superfine) sugar
small wedges of lime, orange and
grapefruit, to garnish

1 Squeeze the juice from the fruits. Some fruit pulp should be used, but discard the seeds.

2 Pour the mixture into a large jug (pitcher). Add the water and sugar. Stir until all the sugar has dissolved.

3 Chill for at least an hour before serving with ice and extra fruit wedges. The drink will keep for up to a week in a covered container in the refrigerator.

Nutritional information per portion: Energy 96kcal/408kJ;
Protein 0.4g; Carbohydrate 25g, of which sugars 25g;
Fat 0.1g, of which saturates 0g; Cholesterol 0mg;
Calcium 17mg; Fibre 0g; Sodium 7mg; Alcohol 0g.

Coffee-chocolate Soda

This is a fun, refreshing drink that tastes as good as it looks. The combination of chocolate ice cream and coffee-flavoured fizz makes for an unusually textured but exciting cocktail.

MAKES 2 GLASSES

250ml/8fl oz strong cold coffee
60ml/4 tbsp double (heavy) cream,
   or 30ml/2 tbsp evaporated
   milk (optional)
250ml/8fl oz cold soda water
2 scoops chocolate ice cream
chocolate-covered coffee beans,
   roughly chopped, to garnish

1 Pour the coffee into tall glasses. Add the cream or evaporated milk, if using. Add the soda water and stir.

2 Gently add a scoop of ice cream. Garnish with the roughly chopped chocolate-covered coffee beans. Serve with a long spoon or a straw.

VARIATIONS
Try chocolate mint, vanilla, hazelnut or banana ice cream and sprinkle with chocolate shavings, fruit slices or even a few roughly chopped pieces of hazelnut.

Nutritional information per portion: Energy 257kcal/ 1060kJ; Protein 2.5g; Carbohydrate 8.9g, of which sugars 8.9g; Fat 23.7g, of which saturates 14.6g; Cholesterol 41mg; Calcium 65mg; Fibre 0g; Sodium 37mg; Alcohol 0g.

Chilled Coffee Caribbean

*Use coffee that is not too
strong in this cold coffee
cocktail. Filter coffee is the
best option as it gives a clean,
clear texture. This recipe
serves two.*

MAKES 2 GLASSES

600ml/1 pint strong filter coffee,
   cooled for about 20 minutes
half an orange and half a lemon,
   thinly sliced
1 pineapple slice
sugar, to taste
1–2 drops of Angostura bitters (optional)
half-slice of lemon or orange, to garnish

1 Add the cooled coffee to the fruit
slices in a large bowl. Stir and chill in
the freezer for about an hour or
until very cold.

2 Remove from the freezer and stir
again. Remove the fruit slices from
the liquid. Add sugar to taste, and
stir in the bitters, if using.

3 Add three ice cubes per drink to
tall glasses, or whisky tumblers, then
pour over the chilled coffee drink.
Garnish with half-slices of orange
or lemon.

Nutritional information per portion: Energy 14kcal/58kJ;
Protein 0.6g; Carbohydrate 3g, of which sugars 2.1g;
Fat 0g, of which saturates 0g; Cholesterol 0mg;
Calcium 10mg; Fibre 0g; Sodium 0mg; Alcohol 0g.

Champurrada

This popular version of Atole is made with Mexican chocolate. A special wooden whisk called a molinollo is traditionally used when making this frothy drink. The recipe serves six.

MAKES 6 GLASSES

115g/4oz Mexican chocolate
1.2 litres/2 pints water or milk,
 or a mixture
200g/7oz white masa harina
25g/2 tbsp soft dark brown sugar

1 Put the chocolate in a mortar and grind with a pestle until it becomes a fine powder. Alternatively, grind the chocolate in a food processor.

2 Put the liquid in a heavy pan and gradually stir in all the masa harina until a smooth paste is formed. Use a traditional wooden molinollo or a wire whisk for a frothier drink.

3 Place the pan over a medium heat and bring the mixture to the boil, stirring all the time until the frothy drink thickens.

4 Stir in the ground chocolate, then add the sugar. Serve immediately.

Nutritional information per portion: Energy 250kcal/
1048kJ; Protein 6g; Carbohydrate 41.6g, of which
sugars 18.8g; Fat 6.8g, of which saturates 3.5g;
Cholesterol 5mg; Calcium 89mg; Fibre 1.1g; Sodium 30mg;
Alcohol 0g.

Mexican Hot Chocolate

This sumptuous version of hot chocolate relies on the beguiling flavours of almond, cloves and cinnamon for its sweetly spicy appeal. The recipe serves four.

MAKES 4 GLASSES

1 litre/1³/₄ pints full-cream (whole) milk
1 cinnamon stick
2 whole cloves
115g/4oz plain dark (bittersweet)
   chocolate, chopped into small pieces
2–3 drops almond extract

1 Heat the milk gently with the spices in a pan until almost boiling.

2 Stir in the chocolate over a medium heat until melted.

3 Strain into a blender, add the almond extract and whizz on high speed for 30 seconds until frothy.

4 Pour into warmed heatproof glasses and serve immediately.

Nutritional information per portion: Energy 220kcal/924kJ;
Protein 8.1g; Carbohydrate 25.3g, of which sugars 25.1g;
Fat 10.4g, of which saturates 6.4g; Cholesterol 13mg;
Calcium 248mg; Fibre 0.6g; Sodium 88mg; Alcohol 0g.

Cocktail Basics

In this part of the book, we shall find out what props and paraphernalia you need to set up your own professional-looking bartending operation. After detailing the bartender's equipment, and types of glasses and garnishes commonly used, we'll learn how to measure, mix and pour, and how to host a successful cocktail party and avoid any unwanted after-effects.

Bartending equipment

To become a successful cocktail bartender, you will need a few essential pieces of equipment. The most flamboyant and vital is the cocktail shaker, but what you have on hand in the kitchen can usually stand in for the rest. After a while, though, you may find the urge to invest in some specialist pieces of equipment.

Measuring jug

Cocktail shakers usually come with standard measures for apportioning out the ingredients. These may be

BELOW: *Measuring jug and spoon measures*

small cups, or something shaped like a double trumpet, one side of which is a whole measure, the other half. If you don't have one, then use a jug (pitcher) for measuring out the required quantities. The measurements can be in single (25ml/1fl oz) or double (50ml/2fl oz) bar measures. Do not switch from one type of measurement to another within the same recipe.

Measure

Be sure to buy a shaker that comes with a measure, known in American parlance as a 'jigger'. They usually come as a single-piece double cup, with one side a whole measure and the other a half. Once you have established the capacity of the two sides, you will save a great deal of bother apportioning out ingredients in a measuring jug. It also looks a lot more professional than using spoons.

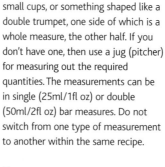

Cocktail shaker

The shaker is used for drinks that need good mixing, but don't have to be crystal-clear. Once the ingredients have been thoroughly amalgamated in the presence of ice, the temperature clouds up the drink. Cocktail shakers are usually made of stainless steel, but can also be silver, hard plastic or tough glass. The Boston

ABOVE: *Measure and cocktail shaker*

shaker is made of two cup-type containers that fit over each other, one normally made of glass, the other of metal. This type is often preferred by professional bartenders. For beginners, the classic three-piece shaker is easier to handle, with its base to hold the ice and liquids, a top fitted with a built-in strainer and a tight-fitting cap. Make sure you hold on to that cap while you are shaking. As a rough rule, the drink is ready when the shaker is almost too cold to hold, which is generally no longer than 15–20 seconds.

Blender or liquidizer

Goblet blenders are the best shape for mixing cocktails that need to be aerated, as well as for creating frothy cocktails or ones made with finely crushed ice. Attempting to break up whole ice cubes in the blender may very well blunt the blades. Opt for an ice bag or dish towel, a rolling pin and plenty of brute force, or better still, use an ice crusher.

Ice bags

These plastic bags that can be filled with water and frozen are a kind of disposable ice tray. You simply press each piece of ice out of them, tearing through the plastic as you go. They also have the advantage of making a more rounded piece of ice, as opposed to the hard-angled cube that an ice tray produces.

Ice crusher

If the prospect of breaking up ice with a hammer and dish towel comes to seem almost as much of a penance as working on a chain gang, an ice-crushing machine is the answer. It comes in two parts. You fill the top with whole ice cubes, put the lid on and, while pressing down on the top, turn the handle on the side. Take the top half off to retrieve the crystals of ice 'snow' from the lower part. Crushed ice is used to fill the glasses for drinks that are to be served frappé. It naturally melts very quickly, though, compared to cubes.

Wooden hammer

Use a wooden hammer for crushing ice. The end of a wooden rolling pin works just as well.

Ice bag or towel

A towel or bag is essential for holding ice cubes when crushing, whether you are creating roughly cracked lumps or a fine snow. It must be scrupulously clean and fresh for each repeated use.

ABOVE: *Ice crusher*

BELOW: *Wooden hammmer and towel*

LEFT: *Blender*

ABOVE: *Ice bucket*

Ice bucket and chiller bucket

An ice bucket with a close-fitting lid is useful if you are going to be making several cocktails in quick succession. They are not completely hermetic though, and ice will eventually melt in them, albeit a little more slowly than if left at room temperature. It should not be confused with a chiller bucket for champagne and white wine, which is bigger and has handles on the sides, but doesn't have a lid. A chiller bucket is intended to be filled with iced water, as opposed to ice alone.

Mixing jug (pitcher) or bar glass

It is useful to have a container in which to mix and stir drinks that are not shaken. The glass or jug should be large enough to hold two or three drinks. This vessel is intended for drinks that are meant to be clear, not cloudy.

Muddler

A long stick with a bulbous end, the muddler is used for crushing sugar or mint leaves, and so is particularly useful when creating juleps or smashes. A variety of sizes is available. It should be used like a pestle in a mixing jug; the smaller version is for use in an individual glass. At a pinch, a flattish spoon

BELOW: *Left to right: muddlers, bar spoon, corkscrew and mixing jug*

can be used instead of a muddler, but then you will find it more awkward to apply sideways rather than downward pressure when trying to press those mint leaves.

Bar spoon

These long-handled spoons can reach to the bottom of the tallest tumblers and are used in jugs, or for mixing the drink directly in the glass. Some varieties look like a large swizzle-stick, with a long handle and a disc at one end. They also look considerably more elegant than a dessert spoon.

LEFT: *Strainer*

LEFT: *Sharp knife*

ABOVE: *Squeezer*

Strainer

Used for pouring drinks from a shaker or mixing jug into a cocktail glass, the strainer's function is to remove the ice with which the drink has been prepared. Some drinks are served with the ice in (or 'on the rocks') but most aren't, the reason being that you don't want the ice to unhelpfully dilute the drink. The best strainer, known professionally as a Hawthorn strainer, is made from stainless steel and looks like a flat spoon that has holes in it and a curl of wire on the underside. It is held over the top of the glass to keep the ice and any other solid ingredients back.

BELOW: *Nutmeg grater*

Corkscrew

The fold-up type of corkscrew is known as the Waiter's Friend, and incorporates a can opener and bottle-top flipper as well as the screw itself. It is the most useful version to have to hand as it suits all purposes. However, the spin-handled corkscrew with a blade for cutting foil is the best one for opening fine wines.

Sharp knife and squeezer

Citrus fruit is essential in countless cocktails. A good quality, sharp knife is required for halving the fruit, and the squeezer for extracting its juice. Although fruit juice presses are quicker to use, they are more expensive and more boring to wash up afterwards.

Zester and canelle knife

These are used for presenting fruit attractively to garnish glasses. If you don't already have them, don't feel obliged to run out and buy them, since drinks can look equally attractive when garnished with simply sliced fruit. The zester has a row of tiny holes that remove the top layer of skin off a

citrus fruit when dragged across it (although the finest gauge on your multi-purpose grater was also designed for just this job). A canelle knife (from the French word for a 'channel' or 'groove') is for making decorative stripes in the skins of a whole fruit. When sliced, they then have a groovy-looking serrated edge. It is, in effect, a narrow-gauged version of a traditional potato peeler, but is purely for decorative purposes.

Nutmeg grater

A tiny grater with small holes, for grating nutmeg over egg-nogs, frothy and creamy drinks. If this sounds too fiddly, buy ready-ground nutmeg instead. It's almost as good.

ABOVE: *Zester and canelle knife*

Straws, swizzle-sticks and cocktail sticks

These decorative items are used to add the finishing touches to a cocktail. It was once considered axiomatic to drink all cocktails through straws. They tend now to be the exception rather than the rule. The flavours of the drink are better appreciated if it is poured directly into the mouth, as opposed to being sucked up in a thin stream. A mythical belief that the alcohol took effect more quickly if taken through straws

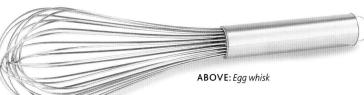

ABOVE: *Egg whisk*

was responsible for their popularity during the 1980s.

A swizzle-stick is useful for stirring a drink, and may be substituted by such food items as a length of whole cinnamon in a short creamy cocktail or a hot, spicy drink such as mulled wine or ale.

Small wooden cocktail sticks (toothpicks) are purely decorative and are generally used for holding ingredients such as cherries or other items of fruit that would otherwise sink to the bottom of the glass. And if you intend to eat the cherry or olive, it's handier if it's already speared, so that you

don't have to commit the appalling *faux pas* of dipping a finger into the drink to catch it.

Egg whisk

Use a whisk to beat a little frothy texture into egg white before you add it to the shaker. It helps to give a better texture to the finished drink. An ordinary balloon whisk will do the trick, although for culinary uses, a rotary whisk with a handle (or the electric specimen) is best.

LEFT: *Swizzle sticks*

BELOW: *Cocktail sticks*

Using a zester

Hold the citrus fruit firmly in one hand and peel away short or long strips of the skin as desired with the other. The pared-away skin makes a delicate garnish that can be scattered over a drink and will float attractively on the surface.

Glasses

To ensure that glasses are sparkling clean, they should always be washed and dried with a glass cloth. Although some recipes suggest chilled glasses, don't put best crystal in the freezer; leave it at the back of the refrigerator instead – an hour should be enough.

Cocktail glass or martini glass

This elegant glass is a wide conical bowl on a tall stem: a design that keeps cocktails cool by keeping warm hands away from the drink. It is by far the most widely used glass, so a set is essential. The design belies the fact that the capacity of this glass is relatively small (about

BELOW: *Cocktail glass*

three standard measures). Uses: the classic martini and its variations, and almost any short, sharp, strong cocktail, including creamy ones.

Collins glass

The tallest of the tumblers, narrow with perfectly straight sides, a Collins glass holds about 350ml/12fl oz, and is usually used for serving long drinks made with fresh juices or finished with a sparkling mixer such as soda. This glass can also stand in as the

BELOW: *Collins glass*

ABOVE: *Liqueur glass and tumbler*

highball glass, which is traditionally slightly less tall. Uses: Tom Collins, and all drinks that are to be 'topped up' with anything.

Old-fashioned glass, tumbler or rocks glass

Classic, short whisky tumblers are used for shorter drinks, served on the rocks, and generally for drinks that are stirred rather than shaken. They should hold about 250ml/ 8fl oz. Uses: Sours and short, whisky-based drinks etc.

Liqueur glass

Tiny liqueur glasses were traditionally used to serve small measures of unmixed drinks, and hold no more than 80ml/3fl oz. They are a good alternative for making a pousse-café or layered cocktail. They are best not used for serving measures of fortified wines, such as sherry, port and Madeira, where they will serve to look ridiculously mean.

Brandy balloon or snifter

The brandy glass is designed to trap the fragrance of the brandy in the bowl of the glass. Cupping the glass in the palm of the hand further helps to warm it gently and release its aromas. Not now considered the thing to use for best cognac, it nonetheless makes a good cocktail glass for certain short, strong drinks that have been stirred rather than shaken. The wide bowl makes them suitable for drinks with solids floating in them.

Large cocktail goblet or poco

Available in various sizes and shapes, large cocktail goblets are good for serving larger frothy drinks, or drinks containing puréed fruit or coconut cream. Classically, they are the

BELOW: *Brandy balloon*

glasses for Piña Coladas. The wider rims leave plenty of room for flamboyant and colourful decorations.

Champagne flute

The champagne flute is the more acceptable glass to use for quality sparkling wines. It is more efficient at conserving the bubbles since there is less surface area for them to break on. It should be used for champagne cocktails too. Always choose one with good depth, as the shorter ones look too parsimonious.

BELOW: *Large cocktail glass*

Champagne saucer

The old-fashioned saucer glass may be frowned on now for champagne, but it is an attractive and elegant design and can be used for a number of cocktails, particularly those that have cracked ice floating in them. Because of the wider surface area, there is plenty of scope for fruity garnishes too.

Red wine glass

The most useful size of wine glass, the red wine glass holds about 500ml/ 16fl oz. It should only be filled about

BELOW: *Champagne flute*

RIGHT: *Red wine glass*

BELOW: *Champagne saucer*

a third full to allow the wine to be swirled around, so that it releases its bouquet. It can be used for long wine cocktails too, and will do at a pinch as a stand-in for the large cocktail goblet.

White wine glass

A long-stemmed, medium-sized glass of about 250ml/8fl oz capacity, a white wine glass should be held by the stem so as not to warm the chilled wine or cocktail. Use it for short wine cocktails such as spritzers and wine-based punches.

Shot glass

A tiny glass with a capacity of no more than 50ml/2fl oz, the shot glass is used for those very short, lethally

strong cocktails known as shooters. This is absolutely the only glass to use if you're going to make a shooter. No substitute will be accepted. The glass itself is usually extremely thick, as these drinks are intended to be thrown back in one, and then the glass slammed down on the bar counter. Go for it.

Pousse-café

A thin and narrow glass standing on a short stem, a pousse-café is used for floating or layering liqueurs one on top of the other. If you haven't got one, use a liqueur glass or even an old-fashioned sherry schooner instead. This is not a type of

ABOVE: *White wine glass*

drink you are likely to be making very often. Although they look impressive, the novelty does rather wear off.

RIGHT: *Pousse-café*

BELOW: *Shot glass*

Garnishes

It is far more elegant not to overdress cocktails, otherwise they all too quickly turn into a fruit salad with a drink attached. Less is definitely best. The edible extras suggested on these pages add colour, flavour and visual interest to any glass.

LEFT:
Many kinds of sugar can be added to drinks: soft brown, demerara, dark muscovado, sugar cubes, cane sugar and caster sugar.

FROSTING

To frost glasses with salt, sugar or cocoa gives a simple but effective touch. It is quick and easy, and the drink needs no other decoration.

Salt is absolutely indispensable for frosting the rim of a textbook Margarita, and is normally done with lime juice. For a sweet drink, sugar frosting makes for an appealingly festive look.

Salt
A traditional Margarita should always have salt around the rim of the glass. To do this, rub the rim with a wedge of fresh lime and then dip the glass in fine salt. This example has an additional twist of cucumber rind as a garnish – but try not to over-garnish your drinks. Less is more.

Sugar and syrup
This champagne saucer was dipped into a shallow bowl of grenadine, then dipped into caster (superfine) sugar to create a frosted rim. The grenadine makes the sugar go bright pink. The glass was then placed in the refrigerator so that it was well chilled before being filled.

Sugar and fruit juice
It is possible to frost a glass with any fruit that goes with the drink. For example, this drink consists of Galliano mixed with a variety of fruit juices and coconut cream. The rim of the glass has been dipped in pineapple juice, then covered in a coating of caster (superfine) sugar.

ABOVE: *Oranges*

RIGHT: *Kumquats*

Alternatively, a dark brown frosting of cocoa powder can be applied to a glass for Brandy Alexander, Cara Sposa or any other creamy cocktail flavoured with chocolate, coffee or orange.

To frost a glass, tip the rim of the glass in water, egg white, citrus juice or one of the syrups, and then dip it again in the chosen frosting. The garnish will take on the colour of the liquid.

CITRUS FRUITS

Edible garnishes should reflect the various contents of the cocktail. Citrus fruit is widely used because it is appetizing to look at and can be cut in advance and kept covered in the refrigerator for a day until needed. Whole slices cut halfway through can be balanced on the rim of a highball glass, while half-slices are best used for floating in a cocktail glass. Apple, pear and banana are also suitable, but they do discolour on exposure to the air; dip them in lemon juice first to preserve colour and flavour.

Lemon is probably the most important fruit of all for the bartender. It is handy in everything from a simple gin and tonic to almost any cocktail.

A lime is small enough for you to be able to use whole slices to garnish a sharp-tasting cocktail containing its juice, such as an Iced Margarita.

Orange is indispensable for garnishing not just orange-flavoured drinks, but old-time mixtures of vermouth and spirit, such as Negroni.

Kumquats are bitter little citrus fruits, which are eaten with the skin on. Use half of one on a stick to garnish a cocktail that has some bitter orange flavour in it.

LEFT: *Lemons*

ABOVE: *Limes*

A twisted half-slice of lemon adds an elegant decoration to any cocktail containing lemon juice.

A simple twist of lime looks effective and adds to the taste of a tequila, banana and lime cocktail.

Grated orange rind goes well with drinks containing orange, such as this creamy chocolatey-orange Tuaca and orange curaçao cocktail.

SOFT FRUITS

Fresh soft fruit such as strawberries, cherries, peaches, apricots, blackberries and redcurrants make fabulous splashes of colour and add a delicious flavour to drinks, although they still tend to be mainly available in the summer.

Quartered large strawberries or, better still, the whole, small, wild variety, such as the French fraises des bois, would look good on a Frozen Strawberry Daiquiri.

Whole fresh cherries, particularly the black varieties, can be used in place of standard cocktail cherries from a jar to adorn a drink containing cherry brandy or kirsch. Singapore Sling contains the former, Rose the latter. The maraschino cherry is a popular option too, even though it is seen as something of a cliché these days.

A thin slice of ripe peach is appropriate for a drink containing peach schnapps or peach brandy, such as Sparkling Peach Melba. White peach is best.

If there's apricot brandy in the drink, a thin slice of apricot will work well. Use only the juiciest, ripest fruits though. The French Bergeron is a good variety.

The endless supply of tropical fruits available all year long, such as mango, pineapple, star fruit, papaya, physalis and the various types of melon, offers numerous decorative ideas and

ABOVE: *Strawberries*

combinations for garnishing. A twiglet of redcurrants, perhaps with a little sugar frosting, makes a rather Christmassy-looking garnish. Physalis is a favourite garnish for modern desserts. Bring it into the cocktail repertoire too for exotically flavoured drinks.

Using soft fruits
A cherry and an apricot slice can be skewered with a cocktail stick (toothpick) to make a stylish, fruity garnish.

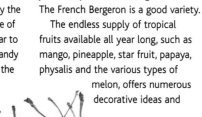

ABOVE: *Cherries*

BELOW: *Peaches*

BELOW: *Physalis*

OTHER GARNISHES

Not all garnishes and decorations need be fruit. A block of chocolate can be grated over a drink, or melted and scraped into chocolate curls, to decorate a cocktail such as Irish Chocolate Velvet.

Ground (or whole) cinnamon is an appropriate garnish for hot mulled wine or punch.

Nutmeg goes well with egg-nogs and flips. Either grate whole nutmegs, or add the powdered version to the surface of cream cocktails containing chocolate or coffee flavours. A Brandy Alexander cries out for nutmeg.

To some, green olives are indispensable in a dry martini; to others, they are anathema. When

LEFT: *Green and black olives*

BELOW: *Nutmeg*

LEFT: *Cherry tomatoes*

martinis do call for a green olive, always opt for those packaged in brine, not in oil.

Plain or chilli-pepper vodka can stand up to pickled chillies, while red chillies should set the palate alight in a drink containing pepper vodka.

Cherry tomatoes are an interesting alternative for garnishing a Bloody Maria, while celery can be the swizzle-stick.

As well as forming an integral ingredient in some cocktails, a sprig of fresh mint makes an appealing garnish to mint-flavoured drinks.

BELOW: *Chocolate*

LEFT: *Red chillies*

LEFT: *Mint*

ABOVE: *Celery*

Using other garnishes

A sprig of fresh mint adds freshness to drinks such as Long Island Iced Tea, or anything containing crème de menthe.

Grated dark chocolate adds flavour to sweet cocktails such as this gin, banana and cream mixture.

Whole cinnamon sticks can be used as stirrers for hot drinks such as coffee or hot chocolate.

Tricks and techniques of the trade

It is worth mastering the techniques for the preparation of good-looking drinks. The following pages give you precise directions for some of the essential procedures, such as crushing ice, as well as some not-so-essential skills, such as making decorative ice cubes. Mastering these tricks is what will distinguish the dedicated bartender from the amateur dabbler.

CRUSHING ICE

Some cocktails require cracked or crushed ice for adding to glasses, or a finely crushed ice 'snow' for blending. It isn't a good idea to break ice up in a blender or food processor as you may damage the blades.

1 Lay out a cloth, such as a clean glass cloth or dishtowel, on a work surface, and cover half of it with ice cubes. (If you wish, you can also use a cloth ice bag.)

2 Fold the cloth over and, using the end of a rolling pin or a wooden mallet, smash down on the ice firmly, until you achieve the required fineness.

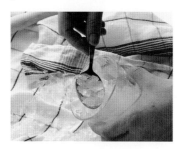

3 Spoon the ice into glasses or a jug (pitcher). Fine ice snow must be used immediately because it melts away like morning mist, but cracked or roughly crushed ice can be stored in the freezer in plastic bags. Stay up all night with a sledgehammer, and you should have enough to do a moderate-sized social gathering. Alternatively, just buy an ice crusher.

MAKING DECORATIVE ICE CUBES

Decorative ice cubes can instantly jolly up the simplest of cocktails. Flavour and colour the water with fruit juices or bitters, and freeze in three stages.

1 Half-fill each compartment of an ice cube tray with water and place in the freezer for 2–3 hours, or until the water has frozen.

2 Prepare the fruit, olives, mint leaves, lemon rind, raisins or borage flowers and dip each briefly in water. Place in the ice-cube trays, put in the freezer and freeze again.

3 Top up the trays with water and return to the freezer to freeze completely. Use as required.

FROSTING GLASSES

Both the appearance and taste of a cocktail are enhanced if the rims of the glasses are frosted. You can use a variety of ingredients, such as celery salt, grated coconut, grated chocolate, coloured sugars or unsweetened cocoa powder for an eye-catching effect. Once it is frosted, place the glass in the refrigerator to chill until needed, if you have time.

1 Hold the glass upside down, so the juice does not run down the glass. Rub the rim of the glass with the cut surface of a lemon, lime, orange or even a slice of fresh pineapple. You can aso use egg white for the frosting liquid, instead of fruit juice, if you like.

2 Keeping the glass upside down, dip the rim into a shallow layer of sugar, coconut or salt.

3 Redip the glass, if necessary, and turn it so that the rim is well-coated.

4 Stand the glass upright and allow it to sit until the sugar, coconut or salt has dried on the rim. Chill the frosted glass until you are ready to use it.

SHAKING COCKTAILS

Cocktails that contain sugar syrups or creams require more than just a stir; they are combined and chilled with a brief shake. Remember that it is possible to shake only one or two servings at once, so you may have to work quickly in batches. Always use fresh ice each time. Never shake anything sparkling, whether it is cheap lemonade or best-quality champagne, as it will flatten.

1 Add four or five ice cubes to the cocktail shaker and pour in all the ingredients.

2 Put the lid on the cocktail shaker. Hold the shaker firmly in one hand, keeping the lid in place with the other hand.

3 Shake the ingredients vigorously in the cocktail shaker for about 15 seconds to blend simple concoctions, and for about 20–30 seconds for more complex recipes or drinks that contain sugar syrups, cream or egg. After shaking for the specified amount of time, the cocktail shaker should feel extremely cold to the touch, and the drink inside will be ready to serve.

4 Remove the small cap from the shaker and pour the drink into the prepared glass, using a strainer if the shaker is not already fitted with one.

MAKING TWISTS

As an alternative to slices of fruit, many drinks are garnished with an attractive twist of orange, lemon or lime rind. The most famous cocktail to have this garnish is Horse's Neck, but twists are useful in many other recipes. The twist should be made before the drink itself is prepared, so that you don't keep a cold cocktail waiting.

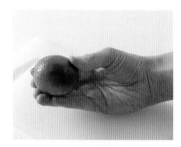

1 Choose an orange, lemon or lime that has an unblemished skin and a regular shape.

2 Using a canelle knife or potato peeler, and starting at the tip of the fruit, start peeling carefully round, as though you were peeling an apple.

3 Work slowly and carefully down the fruit, being sure to keep the pared-away rind in one continuous strip.

4 Trim it, if necessary, to a length that suits the glass.

MELON BALLING

A clever gadget exists for producing perfect little balls of melon that can be used to decorate a cocktail. Choose ripe melon by its fully developed skin colour, which should be properly deep.

1 Cut the ripe melon in half, and scoop out the seeds with a dessert spoon.

2 Push the baller deeply into the flesh of the fruit, and then turn it through 360° to extract as near to a perfect sphere as you can.

3 Thread balls of different-coloured melon (e.g. Galia, Charentais and watermelon) on to a cocktail stick (toothpick) to achieve the most impressive visual impact.

MUDDLING

A muddler – a long stick with a bulbous end – is the only piece of equipment to use for pressing the juice out of mint leaves. This is for use in cocktails in which the mint is an ingredient, rather than where it is a garnish. Muddling is a vigorous process that involves more force than any other technique apart from ice-smashing.

1 Put the mint leaves and caster (superfine) sugar or sugar syrup in the bottom of your glass.

2 Give the mint leaves an initial twist and turn with the muddler to break them up and start mixing them into the sugar.

3 Press the sugar and mint leaves forcefully, with vigorous and repeated turns of the wrist, to fully extract their juices.

FLAMING SUGAR FOR ABSINTHE

This technique of adding a sugar cube to your absinthe is the one favoured by the Czechs. It is much more dramatic than simply pouring water over it, as is the Parisian fashion, and is actually far more efficient anyway.

1 Place a sugar cube on a perforated spoon and immerse it in a generous shot of absinthe until saturated.

2 Balancing the spoon across the top of the glass, use a match to set fire to the sugar cube.

3 As the sugar cooks, the flame will gradually die down, and when it does, gently lower the melting cube once more into the drink, and stir it in to dissolve it.

4 Add the same quantity of cold water as absinthe, and stir the drink once more. It's all a bit of a fuss, but worth it.

MAKING BASIC SUGAR SYRUP

A sugar syrup can sometimes be preferable to dry sugar for sweetening cocktails, since it blends immediately with the other ingredients. Home-made sugar syrup is a useful standby ingredient, and cheaper than buying syrup de gomme. This recipe makes about 750ml/1¼ pints.

350g/12oz caster (superfine) sugar
600ml/1 pint water

1 Place the caster sugar in a heavy pan with the water and heat the mixture gently over a low heat. Stir the water and sugar mixture using a wooden spoon until the sugar has dissolved completely.

2 Brush the sides of the pan with a pastry brush dampened in water, in order to remove any remaining sugar crystals that are stuck to the pan and which might cause the syrup to crystallize.

3 Increase the heat to bring the syrup mixture to the boil, then simmer over a medium heat for 3–5 minutes.

4 Skim any scum from the surface of the syrup using a skimmer and when no more appears, remove the pan from the heat.

5 Allow the syrup to cool and then pour it into clean, dry, airtight bottles. It can be stored in the refrigerator for up to one month.

MAKING FLAVOURED SYRUP

Syrup can be flavoured with an endless variety of ingredients: a split vanilla pod, mint leaves or citrus rind, to name just a few examples. Be imaginative and try some more unusual flavours, if you like. Simply boil, and then bottle with the syrup. This recipe makes about 450ml/³/₄ pint syrup.

900g/2lb very ripe soft or stone fruit, washed
350g/12oz caster (superfine) sugar

1 Put the washed fruit of your choice in a bowl.

2 Using the bottom of a rolling pin, a wooden pestle or a potato masher, crush the fruit well to release the juices.

3 Cover and allow to sit overnight to concentrate the flavour.

4 Strain the purée through a cloth bag or piece of muslin (cheesecloth). Gather the corners of the cloth together and twist them tightly, to remove as much juice as possible.

5 Measure the amount of juice and add 225g/8oz sugar to every 300ml/¹/₂ pint fruit juice. Place the pan on a low heat and stir until the sugar has dissolved.

6 Continue as for basic sugar syrup. Store in the refrigerator for up to one month.

MAKING FLAVOURED SPIRITS

Gin, vodka and white rum can be left in a jar with a wide variety of soft fruits, such as strawberries, raspberries or pineapple, for up to one month, where they will steep and absorb the flavours of the accompanying fruit. You can experiment with other soft fruit, depending on what is in season. This recipe makes about 1.2 litres/2 pints of flavoured spirit.

450g/1lb raspberries, strawberries, or pineapple
225g/8oz sugar
1 litre/1³/₄ pints gin, vodka or light rum

1 Put the raspberries, strawberries or pineapple in a wide-necked jar that has a tight-fitting lid and add the sugar.

2 Add the spirit and cover the jar tightly with the lid. Leave in a cool, dark place for a month, shaking the jar gently every week.

3 Strain through clean muslin (cheesecloth) or a cloth bag, and squeeze out the rest of the liquid from the steeped fruit.

4 Return the flavoured liquor to a clean bottle and seal. Store in a cool, dark place. It will happily keep for up to one year.

STEEPING SPIRITS

The process of steeping any spirit with a flavouring agent, such as chillies in this case, creates a whole new taste sensation, which is not to be missed. This recipe makes about 1 litre/1¾ pints.

25–50g/1–2oz small red chillies, or to taste, washed

1 litre/1¾ pints sherry or vodka

1 Using a cocktail stick (toothpick), prick the chillies all over in order to release their flavours.

2 Pack the chillies tightly into a sterilized bottle.

3 Top up with sherry or vodka. Fit the cork tightly and leave in a dark place for at least ten days or up to two months.

Variations for steeping spirits
Try the following interesting alternatives for steeping spirits. The amount of flavouring used is of course a matter of personal taste.

Gin with cumin seeds, star anise or juniper berries.

Brandy with 25g/1oz peeled and sliced fresh ginger, or 15g/½oz whole cloves.

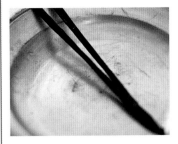

Rum with 2–3 pricked vanilla pods (beans).

Professional bartending

There is much more to becoming a successful bartender than being able to whip up a few cocktails at home. Associations, qualifications and training courses mean this is a skilful and vibrant profession.

The job has something of the nature of a true vocation about it, with national and international professional associations for working bartenders and a constant interchange of information taking place via trade journals and the internet. Educational courses, in both the theory and practice of what has come to be known quite seriously as 'mixology', are organized, and the crowning events of each year are the cocktail competitions, at which aspiring grand masters produce their latest new creations for an international panel of judges.

While there is inevitably an air of commodious bonhomie about such occasions, that does not mean they are not taken extremely seriously. The fact that, when all is said and done, you are dealing in strong alcoholic drink is never forgotten, and there is a focus on encouraging responsible drinking as well as dispensing enjoyment. Achieving a full understanding of the raw materials of your trade – learning the history of each drink, gaining familiarity with its range of flavours and its potential in the mixed drink repertoire – is absolutely essential. New products are coming on to the market at a faster rate than ever before. Some are likely to be here today and gone tomorrow; others are of more lasting importance. They must all become familiar to you.

The approach to cocktail creation must be taken as seriously and as studiously as learning to become

BELOW: *Dealing with a press of thirsty customers can be a thoroughly daunting, but highly enjoyable business.*

ABOVE: *A good bartender needs to know his or her way around a bewildering array of products these days.*

a chef, and indeed there are obvious connections between the two professions. You don't just suddenly become a bartender overnight because you can make a Brandy Alexander that your friends like without spilling anything. The skills you will acquire will include consistency (making sure the same drink turns out tasting the same way each time), dexterity (shaking up one cocktail after another for a bar full of thirsty customers is necessarily lightning-quick and exhausting work), and what is known in the educational courses as 'flair training'.

Putting it roughly, flair training will enable you to withstand comparison to Tom Cruise in the famous 1988 motion picture *Cocktail* (for which the tagline was 'When he pours, he reigns'). Believe it or not, they really

do teach aspiring mixologists how to juggle with bottles, create pyrotechnical effects with flaming alcohol, and even set up little brain-teasers with matchsticks for those, perhaps sitting with their elders in a hotel bar, not quite old enough to drink.

Most countries have professional organizations. The American Bartenders' Guild, and its British equivalent the UKBG, are among the longest-established, and many now belong to an umbrella group called the International Bartenders Association. The IBA was founded with a meeting at the Grand Hotel in Torquay, south-west England, in 1951. Just seven European countries were represented at that inaugural gathering – Denmark, France, Italy, the Netherlands, Sweden, Switzerland and the UK – but the group now claims members from all around the world. It held its first cocktail competition at its 1955 conference, the prize being carried off by an Italian bartender, Giuseppe Neri. In 1975, the IBA took the revolutionary step of admitting female members, and at the beginning of the 21st century, 50 years after its foundation, it now boasts over 50 international affiliates.

If you should feel yourself drawn to this very singular vocation, the first step is to acquire the skills and techniques we have been looking at in this book. Hosting even a small cocktail party, and keeping things flowing without either major spillages or (even worse) running out of ice, is almost as challenging as organizing

army manoeuvres. Only when you have reached an elevated level of aptitude in that department should you go on to the really fun side of the business, namely, inventing your own cocktail recipes.

Useful professional publications to help get you started are the UKBG's *International Guide to Drinks*, or, in the United States, *The Original Guide to American Cocktails and Drinks* (*The Bartender's Companion*). *Class*, 'the magazine of bar culture', is a vibrant and entertaining consumer journal that keeps track of what's going on in fashionable bars around the world. Good websites that are worth a look include *www.cocktailtimes.com* and *www.webtender.com*. Both are full of recipes, as well as containing plenty of invaluable reference information.

BELOW: *A professional barman at work is something of a showman too, entertaining customers with an array of tricks.*

Planning a party

Once you've mastered a few tricks of the trade, it's time to test out your newly acquired flair on a group of friends. This will be the time to see how you cope under pressure, but it will also be fun and rewarding if you manage to pull it off smoothly.

The key to planning and carrying out your first successful cocktail party is to start small. Inviting the entire neighbourhood to a riotous bash might sound rather tempting, but you will only come unstuck by

BELOW: *Nibbles will help absorb some of the alcohol consumed, but try to keep them simple for your own convenience.*

overreaching your own resources. A small group of old friends – say, half a dozen – is a good starting point. Browse through the recipe section of this book, try out for yourself a few of the recipes that appeal to you, and whittle them down to two or three that you think will prove popular with guests whose tastes are familiar to you. A pleasing balance of sour and sweet, or sour, sweet and fizzy, drinks will make for a satisfying evening. Choosing one cocktail that can be made in the liquidizer, one in the shaker and one that is mixed in a jug (pitcher) would make the most logistical sense, so that you are not frantically rinsing out the shaker as guests move from one cocktail to another.

It's a good idea to state your start and end times in advance when you invite people. That way, you can

ABOVE: *Champagne should chill in a bucket of iced water for about 15 minutes.*

ensure that you are not still dealing with thirsty stragglers at one o'clock in the morning.

Provide food, but make it clear that this is a cocktail evening, not a dinner party. You are going to be quite busy enough with drink preparation, without having to cook. However, the more guests are encouraged to eat, the slower the intoxication effect will set in. Little salty and cheesy nibbles, tortilla chips with dips, and nuts are always popular. If you really want to splash out, you could make or buy some canapés ahead of time as well.

Decide on which glasses you are going to use for which cocktail, and make sure there is one of each for each guest. Carefully go through your checklist of vital equipment several times, to be certain you haven't forgotten anything: shaker (with

measures), liquidizer, jug, glasses, fruit for garnishing (remember that citrus fruit slices and twists can be prepared in advance before anyone arrives), a knife for last-minute slicing of fruit, bags of ice, and any special opening implements for flipping off bottle-tops or pulling corks. Serving each drink on a little folded paper napkin is the kind of professional touch that is sure to really impress your guests.

Quantities will depend on how many people you invite, but it is worth doing some initial calculations. A standard measure in these recipes is 25ml/1fl oz, of which there are 28 in a standard bottle of spirits and 20 in a 50cl bottle of liqueur. Divide each bottle not by single

measures, but rather by the number of measures in each recipe, which may be higher or lower than one measure. For some drinks, you may find a half-bottle will be quite enough to be going on with.

ABOVE: *It's a good idea to have your glasses and garnishes prepared beforehand.*

BELOW: *Work out roughly how much of each spirit and liqueur you will need in advance of the party to avoid running out.*

If there is one golden rule, it has to be that you can never have too much ice. Cocktail-making uses an enormous amount of ice, as each batch is only used for the few seconds it takes you to shake the cocktail, and is then thrown away. But remember that ice is only water after all, so be extravagant, and if you aren't sure you have enough ice trays or bags to cope, then buy one of those industrial-sized bags of ice from the supermarket. Better still, buy two or three of them, which shouldn't set you back too much. They aren't very cost-effective, I admit, but at some late stage in the evening, you'll be mighty glad it's there, if only to clamp firmly on your head as you see the last happy guests away.

So good luck, and have fun!

Alcohol and health

Advice about how much alcohol is safe to consume on a daily basis can be misleading and confusing, with government advice and warnings changing regularly. On the other hand, we are constantly hearing news that alcohol can have positive health benefits too. Here we weigh up the health risks and benefits of alcohol.

It is important to be aware of both the legal and your personal limits when it comes to drinking alcohol. Alcohol is virtually worthless in terms of nutritional value and, if drunk in excess, is positively harmful.

BELOW: *Drinking plenty of water between alcoholic drinks is a good way to slow down the onset of inebriation.*

ABOVE: *Nuts and fruits are efficient sources of essential protein and vitamins to help replace lost nutrients.*

Heavy drinking damages the liver, possibly irreparably, and puts strain on its normal day-to-day functioning. It also depletes nutrients in the body, such as vitamins A and C, the B

BELOW: *Lining your stomach with a glass of milk before you embark on an evening of drinking can help prevent a hangover.*

vitamins, magnesium, zinc and the essential fatty acids, and leads to severe dehydration.

Modern methods of producing alcoholic drinks often mean that your average glass of wine, beer or spirit will contain chemical pesticides, colourants and other noxious additives, which you might be a lot more circumspect about if you found them in food products. There are no laws about labelling these ingredients on alcoholic drinks.

Each drinker famously has his or her own limit. What may be no more than a convivial evening's imbibing to one would have the next person sliding under the table. As a very general rule, an adult woman's capacity is thought to be about two-thirds that of a man's, so women should not feel under any pressure to keep pace.

ABOVE: *The number of units of alcohol in a standard glass of beer or wine may be a lot higher than you realize.*

ABOVE: *A variety of nutritious fruit juices will help to make life fun during periods of abstinence from alcohol.*

ABOVE: *Red wine is thought to have significant health benefits as it contains useful amounts of antioxidants.*

It would be disingenuous to pretend that you won't at some stage wake up feeling so unutterably lousy that you'll swear to forgo all strong liqueurs for evermore. Welcome to the wonderful world of the alcohol hangover, caused by dehydration and too much toxin in the bloodstream. Everybody has his or her own best cure, whether it be milk, fried foods, black coffee, the rather dubious hair-of-the-dog approach (i.e. another small drink) or my own indispensable standby: aspirin.

Far smarter than a hangover cure, though, is knowing how to avoid such a ghastly outcome in the first place. Ways of doing this include: lining the stomach with lactic fat (300ml/ 1/2 pint full cream (whole) milk) before you embark on the evening's

drinking; taking 500mg of aspirin beforehand; downing a glass of water between drinks to rehydrate; and (most important of all) slowly drinking a pint of water before falling into bed.

Treat yourself to a break from it all periodically. Non-alcoholic juices made from fruits and vegetables stimulate the body, speed up the metabolism, encourage the elimination of toxins through the lymphatic system, and strengthen the body's overall immunity. They play a vital role in detoxing – everyone's favourite pastime in January – and should be drunk fresh. When making juices at home, choose ripe fruits and vegetables. Fresh juices can be very strong, so dilute them with filtered or mineral water to taste. They should always be drunk as

soon as they are made to ensure you get the maximum benefit from the nutrients.

Health food stores and pharmacies sell a natural remedy called milk thistle in capsule form, which has been clinically proven to assist in liver cell regeneration. Take it in doses of up to 200mg per day, especially during periods of abstinence. It really will make you feel better.

On the positive side, today it is commonly thought that a glass of wine a day can be good for you. It is a bulwark in the body's defence against coronary heart disease because its antioxidants help to break down bad cholesterol in the arteries. To some extent, alcohol in any of its forms can assist in this, but the risks of alcohol consumption should not be forgotten.

Glossary

What follows is a list of the generic terms most frequently encountered in the cocktail world.

ABV: Stands for 'alcohol by volume', and shows the total percentage within the drink that is accounted for by pure ethyl alcohol. All alcoholic products must, by law, give this information.

Aperitif: Any drink taken before eating as a stimulant to the appetite. Can be as simple as a glass of dry white wine, champagne or sherry. Can also be a dry or sour cocktail.

Chaser: A longer drink that is taken immediately after a small one, typically a glass of beer to follow a shot of neat spirit. It soothes the throat after the high alcohol of its predecessor.

BELOW: Champagne, on its own or in a cocktail, is an excellent aperitif for whetting the appetite before a meal.

Cobbler: A long drink consisting of spirit with sugar and ice, served with plenty of fruit to garnish. American in origin, it is the forerunner of all lavishly garnished cocktails.

Collins: A long drink originally called the Tom Collins after a particular variety of gin. A Collins is now any spirit mixed with lemon juice and sugar, and topped up with soda. It is basically a long version of the Sour.

Cooler: An indeterminate long drink that consists of any spirit with fruit juice (usually citrus), sugar and a sparkling topper (which may be soda, lemonade or ginger ale). Classically decorated with a spiral citrus twist.

Crusta: Any drink that comes in a glass with a frosted rim, usually of sugar (although the salt-rimmed Margarita is theoretically a Crusta too). Should also technically be served with a continuous twist of lemon rind lining the glass.

Cup: Essentially the cold version of Punch, a Cup is a mixture of wine or cider with spirits and fruit juices, served from a large bowl full of fruit garnishes and ice. Best served in summer.

Daisy: A soured spirit that also contains a measure of fruit syrup such as grenadine, topped up with soda.

Egg-nog: A long mixture of spirit or fortified wine with egg, sugar and milk, served cold and seasoned with nutmeg. Traditional at Christmas in the USA.

ABOVE: A Cup makes a refreshing, long drink as a party starter. They are generally lavishly garnished with fruit.

Fix: Virtually the same thing as a Daisy. Consists of spirit, lemon juice, a fruit syrup and a sparkling topper, but with the Fix, it is essential to put the squeezed lemon rind into the drink.

Fizz: Almost any long drink topped up with soda, but classically just spirit, lemon juice, sugar and soda, perhaps with a drop of egg white to help the texture. Buck's Fizz, a champagne drink, marked a radical departure for the Fizz.

Flip: A short drink containing egg, sugar and either spirit or fortified wine, usually seasoned with nutmeg. Like an egg-nog, but without the milk.

Frappé: Any drink that is served over a snow of finely crushed ice.

Highball: Simply spirit with ice, topped up with soda or other sparkling mixer, but with no other ingredient.

Julep: A hot-weather American drink, served in a tall glass. Consists of spirit (classically bourbon) and plenty of crushed ice, on a base of mint leaves pressed with sugar. As the ice melts, it becomes a long drink.

Mulling: The technique of gently heating wine, beer or cider with spices, fruit and perhaps a shot of spirit. To be served hot during the British Christmas season.

Neat: Any spirit drunk on its own without ice or mixer. 'As it comes' is the synonymous phrase.

On the rocks: Any drink served over ice cubes or cracked ice, usually in a tumbler or Old-fashioned glass.

Pick-me-up: Any drink whose purpose is to revive the drinker, whether in mid-morning or to

BELOW: This pousse-café is attractively layered with Kahlúa, Bailey's Irish Cream and Grand Marnier.

counteract the effects of over-indulgence. It is a bit of a loaded term, since it shouldn't be forgotten that all alcohol depresses the central nervous system, rather than 'picks it up'.

Pousse-café: A small cocktail in which two or more ingredients are poured slowly into the glass one by one to create a layered effect. Must be served without ice or garnishes.

Punch: An old British colonial drink consisting of spirits and wine, heated up with spices and fruit, and served from a large bowl. Similar to mulled wine, and likewise traditionally served at Christmas.

Rickey: A unsweetened measure of spirit with lime juice and ice, topped up with soda.

Sangaree: May be based on a spirit, but is usually fortified wine with sugar, soda and a nutmeg topping.

Shooter: A small, strong cocktail served in a shot glass, intended to be downed in one. Historically, any tot of neat spirit taken in the same way.

Shrub: A drink consisting of spirit (usually brandy or rum) bottled with fruit juices and loaf (or lump) sugar, and left to infuse for several weeks.

Sling: A long drink consisting of spirit with lemon juice, sugar and soda. Similar to a Collins, it now generally contains a shot of some liqueur as well.

ABOVE: A sour is a sharp, refreshing drink made from gin, fresh lemon juice and a pinch of sugar.

Smash: An undersized version of the Julep, made with ground mint, sugar and a spirit. However, it is served in a smaller glass and with not as much ice.

Sour: Any spirit mixed with lemon juice and a pinch of sugar, sometimes taken with a small splash of soda, but always as a short drink.

Swizzle: A cocktail of Caribbean origin involving spirit, lime juice, bitters, sugar and ice, frothed up by being vigorously stirred with a swizzle-stick held between the palms of the hands. Must be served Antarctically cold.

Toddy: A cold-weather drink consisting of spirit, lemon juice and sugar (or perhaps honey), to which hot water is added. This was implicitly believed in as a cold remedy by previous generations.

Index